FRAME BY FRAME

An Animator's Journey

FRAME BY FRAME

An Animator's Journey

Co Hoedeman

AT BAY press

WINNIPEG

Frame by Frame: An Animator's Journey

Design by Matthew Stevens and M. C. Joudrey.
Layout by Matthew Stevens and M. C. Joudrey.

Published by At Bay Press November 2021.

Library and Archives Canada cataloguing in publication is available upon request.

ISBN 978-1-988168-55-5

Printed and bound in Canada.

This book is printed on acid free paper that is 100% recycled ancient forest friendly (100% post-consumer recycled).

We acknowledge the generous support of the Canada Council for the Arts and the Manitoba Arts Council.

Canada Council for the Arts Conseil des arts du Canada

MANITOBA ARTS COUNCIL CONSEIL DES ARTS DU MANITOBA

First Edition

10 9 8 7 6 5 4 3 2 1

atbaypress.com

Dedicated to Frans van Hes
1921 – 2018

Contents

Born in a Dangerous Time

When I first opened my eyes to the light on August 1st, 1940, the country of my birth was in the midst of war. Less than three months earlier, the Nazis had invaded and Holland was under an oppressive occupation. Fighting, bombing and famine would scar The Netherlands for five long years, killing and terrorizing the Dutch people. Our survival during this dangerous time depended on the courage and resourcefulness of my parents, Anna-Maria Holtkamp and Gosen-Jacobus Hoedeman.

My father was a tailor, a trade he learned in my grandfather's atelier in Amsterdam. I would go to visit with Papa and climb the steep stairs to the third floor of my grandparents' house on the Groen Burgwal canal in downtown Amsterdam. There I would help my grandfather (my Opa) pull white threads out of the jackets he was sewing. I can still see him sitting behind the window, perched on the edge of the table in a cross-legged position, (kleermakerszit) like a character in a fairytale, sewing clothes by hand. Later, I would also help pull loose threads for my father's clothing designs. Papa was promoted to 'coupeur', an important job in the clothing business. He would lay out an original fashion design, and transform it into a paper pattern called 'patronen' that would then be cut out and laid on the fabric for further processing.

During the Nazi occupation, my father was forced to make uniforms for the German army, but this clothing wasn't always *prêt-à-porter*! Sometimes he and his colleagues would deliberately cut one leg of the trousers shorter than the other, or sew buttonholes in the wrong places on the uniforms. It was all hush-hush, and the Germans didn't discover the shoddy work until the goods were safely delivered to far-away Germany. Despite making uniforms for the Germans, my father was always at risk of being taken away to a work camp in the infamous round-ups known as Razzias. Starting at one end of the street, German soldiers would go from house to house, flushing out the men between 17 and 40 years of age to work in labor camps. Many of them never returned home.

The houses on our street were all connected, and there were passages in the walls on the attic level that led from house-to-house. The men would avoid capture by escaping through these passages. The Razzias became more frequent as the war came closer to an end. In Rotterdam alone, more than 50,000 men were taken away by truck. As our house was at the end of the street, my father had another way of avoiding detection. By the time the soldiers reached our house Papa was already wedged into a tiny cramped space on the top shelf of the cupboard in the living room. Fortunately, the Nazis never found him.

Helping my father and Opa make clothes with their hands was an experience that I later employed in my film career to create puppets and sets for animation projects. It was also during the Second World War that I had my first encounter with puppets, which would eventually lead to my career in stop-motion animation in Canada. Sometimes I went with my father to the Dam Square to attend puppet shows in the middle of Amsterdam.

There was a portable little puppet theatre that stood in the middle of the open square, with pigeons snooping around, and an ice-cream vendor selling his wares right in front of the Royal Palace of Amsterdam, one of three palaces in The Netherlands at the disposal of the monarch. A small crowd of children were glued to the spot watching every move by the puppeteer hidden inside the little theatre. The show was always the same, with Jan Klaasen bashing the head of Katrijn with his club and the policeman putting an end to it all. These characters were the Dutch equivalent to Punch and Judy. We kids always loved the show even though it was cruel because it was magical and hilarious. At the end of the show, my father would sometimes treat us to ice cream right where the theatre stood. It was all quite wonderful. After the show, life around the Dam Square went on as usual. The trams criss-crossed around us, people went shopping, and the traffic kept going.

When we were older, we moved to Haarlem, a small town just outside of Amsterdam, where we would regularly see puppet shows at the old Town Hall. I saw *Cinderella, Snow White* and many classic children's fables. At a time when there was no television, and little access to any kind of entertainment, puppet shows were the most brilliant experience imaginable. Puppet theatre and puppet animation have a lot in common. The animator and his team, just like the puppet master in a puppet show, is in control of everything: the storyline, the movements, the sets, the puppets, the animation and the emotions of the audience.

Puppets are magical, especially for a young boy. Things can happen that are almost impossible to show in other theatre forms. For me, playing with puppets was an ideal way to learn about movement. Objects can be used to tell stories and their movement can convey emotions. The way something moves can determine the length of a production, slowing it down or speeding it up. It also led to observing how things moved in the world like leaves in the wind, or how various movements of humans are so different. My film, *Marianne's Theatre/Le théâtre de Marianne* (2004) is a direct link to my experiences watching puppet shows. The puppeteer, like the film director, is in full control of the action. Little did I know that these fun early lessons would carry me all through my entire career in animation.

By 1944, things were not going well for the Dutch people, particularly in the western part of the country. The Nazi regime had blocked all transportation of goods and food to and from the cities. Nothing moved. The consequences were disastrous: the National Railway went on strike, it was bitterly cold, and there was very little to eat. One day, my father went to the train tracks on the outskirts of the city with my younger brother Frans to collect potatoes and coals that had fallen from the rail cars. Curfew time was fast approaching and they still had to cycle the long way back home. As Papa walked back to his bike, he saw German soldiers taking it away. With his little bag of coals and some potatoes, he and Frans had to walk all the way home. Life was dangerous in those days.

In the city streets many trees were cut down for firewood. Anything that could provide heat was sacrificed. The wooden blocks between the tramway rail tracks ended up in our little wood stoves. People became so desperate they boiled tulip bulbs to make a meagre soup for supper. It was the only way to survive. Many people were dying of starvation, particularly in Amsterdam. There alone, 20,000 people starved to death. The situation became desperate and people wandered out to the country to find food. It was a time of mass starvation, called the Hongerwinter.

In the film *55 Socks/55 Chaussettes/55 Sokken* (2011), I talk about this dark period of starvation by the Nazis. In 1984, I came across a Dutch poem called "*55 Socks*". It's a touching poem by Maria Jacobs about surviving the Hongerwinter of 1944-45 in The Netherlands. In the story, a Dutch mother is hiding two Jewish girls at her home. There is little to eat and the mother is seeking creative ways to put food on the table. She has an old bedspread and decides to take it apart to turn the yarn into socks. She takes the 55 socks on her bicycle into the countryside to barter for food. There she finds a farmer's wife who agrees to take the socks in return for some food. As she turns to leave she puts her hand in her pocket and finds the 55th sock, and asks the farmer's wife if she would like the extra sock. The farmer's wife says yes, and gives her more food. When the mother asks the wife what she wants the socks for, she tells her she plans to take them apart and turn the yarn into a beautiful bedspread.

I wanted to make this film in black and white to emphasize the unsettling period of the Nazi occupation. At the time, I was fascinated by the silhouette animation films by Lotte Reiniger from Germany, and Michel Ocelot from France. Instead of telling the story with puppetry, I decided to do it in silhouettes. The Dutch have a long tradition called schimmenspel, shadow play, and I was very interested in connecting to this well known tradition as a way of solidarity with the people, exploring the simplicity of the shapes and to stylize them.

I transformed my animation table into a large light-box that would accommodate the cut-out artwork. I did not use top lighting and the animation was done right under the camera setup in my basement studio. Using this method created stark images all in black and white, a time of life and death, and it worked out beautifully well. When I started working on *55 socks*, I had barely any knowledge of the hardships and the difficulty of the Dutch to survive, because as a child growing up in that situation, it was what I thought was normal.

Life in Holland became more and more difficult and my parents needed to find ways to keep us all healthy. My uncle's wife had family in the eastern part of the country, and they offered to help us out. Near the end of the war, I travelled with my aunt on her bicycle from Amsterdam to Twello, a village in the east of the country about 85 km away. I was not even five years old, in poor health and needed to regain my strength. I remember very clearly that on the way to Twello we stopped at a farm for a rest and to get some milk. It was sombre, the day was cold and dark, and it all combined to make that nourishing glass of white milk quite unforgettable.

I stayed with relatives of my uncle's wife on a farm to get well. Meanwhile, my twin brother Ferry stayed with other relatives on a nearby farm. My oldest brother Jos also stayed in the region, but our youngest brother Frans remained at home because he was too young to travel without my parents. Even in the countryside there was soon little left to eat. Then just in time, the Allies dropped food parcels from the sky to feed the hungry population and end this disastrous blockade.

From the lifting of the blockade until the end of the war we used coupons to get food and would eat canned food that came from the sky. One day we children were playing with empty food cans in a field nearby. We threw them high in the air and then tried to hit the cans with a stick. The one who hit the can the furthest was the winner. Unfortunately, one of the cans came flying straight at me and hit my face. It left a big scar on my nose. I still have a faint mark from the accident.

Ferry had to return home to Amsterdam because he became homesick, but I stayed on my aunt's farm until Canadian soldiers liberated the country. What a day that was! I remember very well the arrival of the trucks and tanks crossing the river, The IJssel, in the eastern part of Holland. We stood on a makeshift bridge over a canal welcoming the Liberators. At one point I decided to crawl under the railing of the bridge to better see the Allied soldiers. Suddenly the railing gave way, I lost my footing and fell into the water below. The only thing I remember was seeing the silhouette of a pair of black boots coming towards me in the murky green water. Later, family members told me that I was rescued from drowning by the man in the black boots.

It was May of 1945, I was almost five years old and the war was over! As a young child I had no clue what was going on. For me, the liberation by the Canadians was like a big parade that never ended, but for my dad it was a big deal. As the airplanes were flying over, he stood on the rooftop waving with a big white sheet to welcome the Allies. The neighbourhood people organized all kinds of activities to celebrate our freedom. The celebrations were all over the place. Holland was free again and it was time to celebrate and rebuild the country.

Coming of Age

My parents never talked about the war. It was over, and they had no desire to relive it. My father continued working as a coupeur in the clothing studio that was conscripted during the war by the Germans preparing the patterns for mass production, but he also kept an atelier in the attic for individual clients. My mom stayed home with the kids. I played in the attic of our home with my brothers, and helped my mom with light chores. For me, life had improved a lot.

One day when I was back with my family in Amsterdam, I was playing with my spinning top outside on the street when I noticed one of the neighbour's kids with a brand new stepping scooter. That was something I liked much better than my spinning top, so in exchange for letting the kid borrow my top, he agreed that I could borrow his scooter. It all went fine until I had to negotiate a crack in the sidewalk. As I was trying to jump over the gap, the handlebar hit my mouth hard and broke one of my front teeth. I was too ashamed of myself to tell my mother what happened, so I lied about it. I told her a story about breaking my tooth with the whip of the spinning top. Not long after that, one of my front teeth became infected and needed surgery. For years my mother struggled with me going from one dentist to another. Many times we had to go to the hospital as well. I had several surgeries on my teeth, but that did not help much, and in the end I lost both of my front teeth. For years, I had a big gap in my mouth, and Mama always blamed my spinning top.

Meanwhile, the family grew bigger and bigger. After the first four boys, my sister Ans was born in 1946. She was a very lively, pretty girl. She was followed a few years later by my sister Ria. With her curly hair, she looked quite different from the rest of us. Then came the twins, Hetty and Thea. To top it all off, a little boy, Tonnie (Tom), completed the gang of nine children. Honestly, my mother found it rather difficult to be pregnant again and again, and have that many youngsters underfoot. She blamed it on our doctor and the policies of the church on contraceptives.

Our lives revolved around the Catholic Church. My brother Ferry became a very dedicated altar boy and I sang in the church choir. As a group, we choirboys were often quite mischievous. One time, we tied the surplices together just before the senior members of the choir went up for communion. As they stepped forward, they tripped over each other and created a commotion in the church. Another time, we took the big Gregorian music book and paraded with it on the streets around the church. The church caretaker came out shouting and waving his arms, and that quickly put an end to our little parade.

After our move from Amsterdam to Haarlem in 1950, Ferry and I were very involved in the Boy Scouts. Our Boy Scout headquarters was located in the attic of the local school in Haarlem where we met every week. We city boys learned a lot from the Boy Scout activities and the outings. Once a year we would go camping in the woods, on the dunes near the sea, or on a farm. It was rough, and living in the open air and sleeping in tents was very exciting for young boys like us. We learned to cook our own meals on open wood fires, slept on the hard ground in tents, trained for our achievement badges, played many outdoor games, and went hiking. After two weeks of nature camping, I always came home totally exhausted, but happy.

I loved the activities, being out in nature, and roughing it. It was a far cry from urban life. Camping developed in me a desire to be in the woods or on the water, and explore nature. It was a way of being in touch with my self. It was an experience that I wanted to share with my own children when we went camping in the provincial parks of Ontario and Quebec. The skills acquired while camping in the wild develop confidence and independence. Building a fire can be difficult when the wood is too wet, it can take forever to get the water boiling, and when something is forgotten at home, there is a creative challenge to improvise.

I had to rely on my twin brother a lot. Because he was the elder twin, and more serious than I was, my mother held him more responsible for our actions. He was always in charge. One of our chores was to go to the butcher shop to get cold cuts for our lunches. He would make suggestions as to which ones, and I would have to go along most of the time with his decisions. I began to treat my life as a game, turning the challenges into fun experiences. My uncle had given my parents some miniature stone blocks used in construction sites, and as I did not have any building blocks to play with, I used them to build all kinds of structures. This attitude has served me well throughout my life and career.

After the war, my father worked for a number of clothing companies in different Dutch cities, so the family moved from Amsterdam to Haarlem, and later to 's-Hertogenbosch and Apeldoorn. My father preferred women's fashion, although he was very good at making men's clothing. In his own atelier in the attic, he made all the suits for the five boys and dresses for the four girls, including wedding dresses. For many years there was a caricature poster mocking German soldiers attached to the wall in his atelier. I would often stare dreamily at the sausage-eating, fat Germans on the poster. Much later I found out that my younger brother Frans had kept the poster. As a young man, Frans followed in the footsteps of my father and grandfather. He studied fashion and became a fashion designer; something my father always wanted to be, but lacked the education.

My mother was mostly busy with my younger siblings, and she often asked me to do the dishes or sweep the bedroom floors and do other chores. I would sit on the floor in the attic with a large bag full of potatoes and peel them one by one until there were forty in the pot. In those days we did not have automatic washing machines, dishwashers and other conveniences, everything was done by hand. This sometimes created friction between us as I was always looking for an escape to play with my friends on the street, but my brothers and I had to chip in by peeling potatoes, vacuuming floors, washing dishes, getting groceries, or by helping do the laundry by hand.

As a child, I always made things by hand. I was very playful. We built our own little puppet theatre and performed shows with drawings that we drew on cardboard and then cut the perforated images that we projected on the walls. When I talk about we, I mean Ferry, my twin brother and me. Storytelling was one of our favourite pastimes. We built kites, built radio sets, model airplanes and played doctor. With left-over textiles my dad brought home, we built tents and did many other activities. Unknowingly, this was preparing me for my future career as a filmmaker. Little did I know how it would influence my film career later on.

I was not a great student in my early years. I had no *zitvlees*, Mama always said, which meant I couldn't sit still. Twice I failed school and had to do my grade over again, much to the chagrin of my mother. It was becoming clear that regular school was not for me. I would have to find my own path in life. It was agreed that I should find a job in Haarlem and continue my studies in the evenings and weekends. I found a job as an apprentice at a printing company that specialized in children's books. At that time I was barely out of school, 15 years old, impressionable, eager to learn and pretty restless. I wanted something more challenging in my work.

One day, my mother came across a newspaper ad by Multifilm, a full-fledged film studio that produced feature films, documentaries, advertising, and news reels for TV. They also had their own laboratory, editing facilities, sound studios and a 'trick-film' studio that did stop-motion animation, titles and special effects. They were looking for a young animator for their trick-film studio. I was already looking for another job and the idea of doing animation for a film company sounded far more interesting than retouching lithographs and sweeping floors at a printing company. Luckily, the film studio was situated just a few blocks away from my home, in the middle of a park. With the ad in my hand I went to apply for the job.

During the interview with the head of the animation studio, Frans van Hes, I showed him my little portfolio and a few drawings. We got along very well and he hired me on the spot. Frans was a very good artist and became my mentor over the nine years we worked together. On Saturdays, while I was studying in Amsterdam, I regularly visited him at his home where we had tea with his wife, Willemieke. There were two other people working at the studio, André de Vries and Gerda Vogel. Their knowledge of animation was rather limited as well. We all learned on the job as we were animating the characters for the film.

Drawing for animation was not easy to master. I spoiled many drawings before I could animate a decent one. It was essential to be able to translate real time into animation timing, so I trained myself to be observant of the way people move. I would sit on the stairs at the railway station studying people coming and going to the waiting trains. Many times I would go to the Stedelijk Museum in Amsterdam and watch film programs from abroad. The experimental films by Norman McLaren and Len Lye I found particularly exciting.

Unfortunately, Multifilm decided to shelve their animation cartoon film plans, but luckily I stayed on with the company making titles, drawing maps and other trick shots for documentary films and theatrical shorts. It was all in black and white, and I loved it. Right away I knew that I preferred making stop-motion animation over cartoon animation. My first animation project was for a title sequence where the Philips logo would write itself onto the screen before the rest of the title faded in. I shot the title sequence in reverse by scraping a small part of the logo away on a glass plate before shooting each frame. Another stop-motion shot was animating police buttons and the insignias to march to a musical melody for a promotional film for the police force. I was pretty proud of my early accomplishments.

In those early days, we had a rather primitive way of animating standard title sequences, using white cork letters. First we prepared the page layouts, then we placed the cork letters one by one on a glass plate to spell the names. I would arrange the cork letters, then carry the full plate to the camera stand. There I carefully placed the plate under the camera on a piece of decorative wallpaper to serve as the background with shadows and all. I would remove the letters one-by-one, shooting a few frames each time, and then run the film in reverse to reveal the page title animation.

The trick film studio was a converted greenhouse at the corner of the building. Every time the local bus drove by, the windows would rattle and the cork letters started dancing. If one or more of the cork letters moved in the process, which happened all too often, I would have to start over. The animation stand we used at Multi-film was built from an old x-ray machine. The camera attachment could be moved vertically on two pillars by hand, or could be moved up and down with a calibrated turning device. It was all very primitive, but it worked.

The film camera we used was an old wooden box Anton Debrie from the beginning of the century. The mechanics inside the camera were made of brass and wood. In order to see the image in the viewfinder you had to look through the film emulsion, as there was no ground glass. Before filming our artwork we would first take some frames to get rid of the exposed film and then start the shot. This antique camera now sits in the Film Museum in Amsterdam. Needless to say, making titles for film has drastically changed over the years. All this took place before we had Letraset. Now it is all done in moments on any laptop computer.

I also worked with a variety of other film cameras, again each one requiring me to look through the film emulsion, but in slightly different ways. The Parvo L was similar to the Anton Debrie camera, but more advanced as it had the advantage of sliding away the film stock at the back of the lens, replacing it by a ground glass to better see the image through the view finder. With the Askania, a camera frequently used in Eastern Europe, in order to see the image you put a separate piece of film in the film gate and then by looking through the view-finder you could see the image on the film.

Hiring practices in the mid-1950s were very different from what they are today. Back then, when you hired someone it was for a full-time job that could last for life. As a full-time employee, my duties varied depending on the company's needs. Aside from drawing maps and titles for films, I sometimes went out on location as a camera assistant with film, news and documentary crews. At the end of a shooting day, I would take the exposed film rolls, put them in my pocket and take the train to deliver them to the laboratory in Hilversum, a thirty-minute train ride away.

Sometimes the Dutch have unconventional ways of expressing humour. At times, it can be very crude. Once during lunchtime while I was raking leaves in the garden of the studio, the camera crew kidnapped me, bound me to the top of the company van, and drove off to the film location for their next assignment. Being bound to the top of the car was scary, especially in traffic. Fortunately, the rope they used to bind me was loose and I was able to free myself. Climbing back inside through the window of the moving car made the trip a lot safer, and made me feel a lot better too. This was my initiation to the film world as a camera assistant.

Another time, on a rainy day, they asked me to go to Polygoon, another film company nearby, to get a film perforator. Polygoon was famous for its newsreel productions for theatre and television. Back at the studio, with big smiles on their faces they gave me a carefully wrapped parcel that could only be opened in the darkroom. I cycled back to the studio where I went straight to the darkroom to open the parcel. It smelled pretty bad and when I attempted to open the box in the dark, there was nothing but a stinking pile of horse droppings coming out of the box. I should have known better. In reality, the film perforator did not exist. Outside the darkroom door there was a lot of noise and laughter. This must have been hilarious, but not for me. I closed the box, and threw the parcel back at the laughing spectators.

In the late fifties, the Dutch film industry was rather small compared to other countries like the U.K., France or U.S.A. However, the Dutch were very well known for their short experimental films and documentaries. A good example is the film *Glass* (1958), by Bert Haanstra. *Glass* was made as a short experimental film for a longer documentary about glass blowing. It won an Oscar for best documentary short film. Actually, it is one of my favourite films of all time.

As for commercial animation, the Dutch animation studios did quite well, especially abroad. However, independent animation filmmaking did not exist at that time in Holland. In 1958-59, Mulitfilm and Polygoon Profilti merged to become Cinecentrum, and was able to offer greater services and take on much bigger projects. At that time, many small companies were merging into larger ones. The studio in Haarlem continued as the base as we gradually moved the studio to Hilversum over two months. When it was my turn to locate to Cinecentrum in Hilversum, it meant leaving my parents' home.

Moving out was easy and moving to Hilversum was no big deal. I had many contacts and people helping me. Actually, I was looking forward to becoming more independent. No more obligations at home to please my mom. It became the end of an era. I had grown up and was ready to move on.

Making It

In Holland, when moving from one city to another you have to let the bureaucrats know that you are moving out and relocating. Then you have to register in the new town. The difficulty was finding a place to stay. Accommodations were controlled according to the number of people renting. For instance, a single person could not rent a place that would accommodate three people. To know of an available place for rent was usually by word of mouth, as well as ads in the paper. For a while I roomed with my uncle in Haarlem. When I moved to Hilversum, I was lucky and my colleagues recommended a room in the centre of town.

An elderly Portuguese woman had a room for rent right in the old centre of town. It was a grim street, with no cafés or restaurants, or pretty flowers, just row houses. The room was so small there was just enough space for a bed, a small desk and a kerosene heater. I did not know it at that time, but the little heater released some very toxic fumes that sometimes made me feel sick. The walls and the windows were always fogged up. As I was finishing my photography course at that time, I spent a lot of time studying in that room. I had no idea how dangerous the place really was. The old lady also had a daughter with whom she was occasionally fighting. One night after I had just gone to sleep, there was a lot of noise coming in from my little balcony. Sure enough, it was the daughter climbing onto the balcony to my room. She had been locked out of the house and wanted back inside. Despite their fights, they were kind people and the atmosphere was mostly pleasant.

While working at the film studio, I attended the School for Creative Arts (Kunstnijverheidschool) in Amsterdam. I also took weekend classes and correspondence courses at the School of Photography (Fotovakschool) in The Hague, and continued my secondary education in Hilversum. In the early sixties, every able-bodied person was obliged to serve in the army for two years. After my basic training, I applied for the Photo and Film Unit hoping they would exempt me. We were in the middle of final exams when an officer came into the room and announced that I would be promoted to sergeant and be posted to the film unit in The Hague. I was elated.

The two years I spent in the army were like a huge vacation. I had a lot of freedom at the Photo and Film Unit. No more training exercises and typing lessons. Instead, I worked in the laboratory developing films, cutting negatives and lining up soundtracks with the images. Now and then, I would go on location as a camera assistant. I remember going to a military training camp on the island of Vlieland in the north of the country where we filmed night-time shooting exercises at sea. The targets were old abandoned army tanks that were dumped in the shallows. I sat in a real army tank, it was very tight and there was little room to maneuver. During the shooting exercises, it was spectacular to see the flames reflecting on the water as they flew over the derelict tanks.

Sometimes I went with my friend and fellow soldier Jan Boon on his bike from his parents' home in The Hague to the beach in Scheveningen. One day, the military police stopped us. Being a sergeant, I was supposed to be sitting on the back of the bicycle rather than on the front, doing the pedalling. Also, we were not properly dressed, as we were not wearing our berets. We got away with a warning.

One evening, I was on duty as sergeant of the guards. A nice young lady came to the gate and wanted to visit her boyfriend who was detained in the little jail. I was not supposed to let her in, but I felt pity for her and sneaked her inside the cell. At that very moment the night officer came into the barracks to do his rounds. In a little panic, I ran inside the cell block to warn the girl, but she had already found an empty cell to hide in. When the night officer walked inside the cell units I tried to distract him by talking very fast and loud. He did not notice anything out of the ordinary and left. A little shaken up by the event, I quickly opened the cell door and gave the girl her freedom back. The visit with her boyfriend ended up lasting only a few minutes.

During my time in the military, my twin brother Ferry was serving in the Air Force Radar Unit. His service in the army was not a happy time. He often had difficulties with the authorities and opposed following orders. For this rebellion against his superiors, he was regularly not allowed to go home for weekends. Luckily, Ferry found an outlet for his creativity: to repaint the dining hall with a mural of some air force activities. One unfortunate evening while he was walking with a friend on the side of the road on his way to the barracks, a car hit his friend who was killed instantly. Ferry was very traumatized by this, and it had a profound effect on him that lasted for many years. My eldest brother Jos served a much happier time in the marines. A large part of his service, about two years, was spent overseas in Dutch Guinea. When he came home, he looked very tanned and healthy. Frans being the youngest did not have to serve in the army, which only took three conscripts from a family.

While I was fulfilling my two-year military service at the Photo and Film Unit in The Hague, I also finished my studies as a photographer at the School of Photography. On Saturdays, I was able to practice photography with a friend in the old Profilti film studio. We photographed musical instruments and did portrait photography with girls we picked up on the street. Some of the girls were looking for more adventures, but I was too naive to do anything but make portraits. I was relieved to show them out of the studio.

At the time that I graduated from the School of Photography in the Netherlands, we did not have big graduation ceremonies or celebrations like here in Canada. Graduating at that time was no big deal. It just happened. Everything was very modest and I had to pick up my diploma at the school. I continued to focus on my job as a camera assistant in the military, and I was elated it was all over.

After my military service, I went back to Cinecentrum to continue working at the animation studio. By now they were doing a lot of commercial work, and my help was very much needed. It was a pleasure to be among my peers again. Besides earning a little more money, management gave me much more freedom and more responsibilities. At the time, we did a lot of model work for documentary films as well as stop-motion animation for television commercials. For example, they were building the IJ Tunnel in Amsterdam to make room for the subway. We built models of the underwater pontoons and animated them into the right positions. The model sets were miniature cross cuts of the actual locations where the pontoons were to be placed. We projected light patterns on the models to create the underwater effects. I loved doing this kind of stop-motion animation because it demanded a lot of skill, and I loved the way the animated film looked when it was done. Stop-motion filmmaking had become my passion.

Once, we were doing a commercial for Nevada Wool. I took some strands of wool and started twining them together. Out of that grew a little woolen doll with a wire armature inside. We filmed the action of the doll pulling a string that released a whole pile of woolen balls and exposed the Nevada Wool brand name. Later at the NFB, I applied this idea of a wire puppet to my first film *Oddball/Maboule* (1967). This was my very first attempt at puppetry, and the results looked pretty good.

When the demand for TV commercials increased, the workload got much bigger, but not always more exciting or rewarding. One time, we had to do a commercial for the orange soft drink Fanta. A drop of water had to be animated on the front of the bottle. The shots were never to the liking of the German client. It took us four months to have the perfect drop of water roll down the bottle in the perfect way. We, and our client, were finally both happy. We also made many beer commercials, particularly for Grolsch beer. Vakmanschap is Meesterschap (Workmanship is Mastership) was their slogan. The company gardeners, plumbers and electricians always found an excuse to be around the set when we were working with beer. At the end of each shooting day, we poured the leftover beer into tubs outside the studio for the thirsty gang.

As time went on, I became restless and again wanted to expand my horizons. My ultimate dream was to become an independent animation film director, but there were very few opportunities in Holland. Film schools in Holland did not exist back then, so I could only learn on the job. The only studio I knew of that specialized in stop-motion film making was the Joop Geesink Dollywood Studio in Amsterdam, but I did not like their style, and I heard the working conditions weren't great, so I never applied there. Getting subsidies and government grants was next to impossible, and starting my own company out of the question.

A Dutch delegation of animators went to the first animation festival, Les journées International de film d'animation, in Annecy, France. They came back with high praise for Canadians who were honoured at the festival, like the pioneer filmmaker Norman McLaren, and producers Wolf Koenig and Bob Verrall who were in charge of the animation studio at the National Film Board of Canada in Montreal. When I heard about the encounter with the Canadians, I became very excited and wanted to jump across the ocean to join them. I would often go to the film museum in Amsterdam and follow lectures on Canadian filmmaking. In particular, films by Norman McLaren such as *Blinkety Blank*, *V for Victory*, *Neighbours*, and *Canon*, intrigued me a lot. I thought Canada was the place to be for experimental filmmaking. A country with vast spaces and wide horizons sounded so promising.

In the meantime, I fell in love with a wonderful girl, Dukke van der Werf, whom I met at a dance party. After courting her for two years, we were married in 1964. In Holland, there is both a civil ceremony and a religious ceremony. They are separate events with the civil ceremony being the most important one. The wedding was a simple event that was celebrated mostly with family and some friends. Dukke's family are simple people, originally from Friesland. My father made her wedding dress and she helped him with its design. Most weddings in Holland are family affairs. We had the reception at home and we received many presents. As well as dancing, our relatives sang and acted out sketches.

After the wedding, we settled in the town of Hilversum. Because of the housing shortage, it took some effort to find a place, but we managed to rent the upper floor of a townhouse from a very nice lady. Fortunately, Dukke and I had similar taste and styles that made life a lot easier. We had decided to postpone our honeymoon as we were both busy with work. The next summer, we took our honeymoon in France. We took the train to Paris, and hiked in Auvergne, a very old volcanic plateau in the middle of France. We camped in the wild next to a lake. One day while we were out hiking, the gendarmerie left a note on our tent telling us that we had to move because it was illegal to camp there. Living in Holland was not that easy, and work opportunities were not there, so after experiencing life in a different country, we started to think about other places we could live. With the smoke from the campfire still stinging our eyes, we decided to leave Holland and immigrate to Canada.

I wrote letters to apply for animation film jobs in Canada, made a show-reel of some of my work, did exams, passed medical tests and got our finances in order. It was time to quit my job. That was hard, I must admit. My boss, Frans van Hes, wanted me to stay believing that I could make a good career in filmmaking in The Netherlands, but I had other plans. Not long ago, his daughter emailed me saying that Frans died on September 06, 2018. He was 97 years old. She had a message from him for me—he asked her to tell me that he always liked my films and was proud of what I had accomplished.

When we left Holland, the twins, Hetty and Thea, were still pretty young, 13 years old. Tom, the youngest brother, was not even a teenager. They came with my parents to the Holland American Line pier in Rotterdam to wave goodbye. I can still see their small bodies standing behind the windows of the barracks waving at us as the boat pulled away from its moorings. To see the harbour and the landscape disappear in the distance was a very emotional moment for me. Leaving all my family and friends behind was heart-breaking and felt like leaving forever. I really thought I would not see my family and friends for many years to come, but we were determined to continue our adventure to a new land. There were other countries we could have chosen, but we preferred Canada.

Crossing the Atlantic Ocean by boat in October of 1965 also had its challenges. We encountered stormy seas and many of the passengers, including us, became seasick. There was a lot of entertainment on the boat, but we were sometimes too sick to take part in it. Taking Gravol helped me a lot, but Dukke had more difficulty coping with seasickness than I did. During the calls for lunch or dinner we met many other passengers from different parts of the world. The lunches and dinners were quite extravagant with lots of choices. During this time, I would often meet Canadians returning home from holidays in Europe. Our small sleeping cabin next to the engine room was very noisy, but it didn't bother us. I would go on deck to watch the waves and the occasional leaping dolphins. I was fascinated by it all, but after nine days at sea, we were glad to see the shores of Labrador come into sight. We had arrived in Canada.

Our first stop was Quebec City. I was in awe seeing the hills lit up in the distance. The boat stayed overnight, and then we began the last leg of our travels on the Saint Lawrence River. When we arrived in Montreal, it looked very impressive and big from a distance. I had never seen a skyscraper in my life. It took a while before we disembarked the boat because the custom officers were very meticulous, but friendly. The language was a mixture of English and French. English was not too difficult to follow, but the French was next to impossible. When people talked, you could hardly see their mouths move. I did not find the people very different from the Dutch, maybe a little more friendlier.

Downtown Montreal was a beehive of activities. Everything was big, something I was not accustomed to. When we arrived, a bus took us to the railroad station. I sat glued to the window to take it all in. From there we were assigned accommodation. The tourist house where we stayed was old and dirty. There was not even a table to prepare our food or read the paper. Dukke was sick and I explored the neighbourhood on my own to get groceries. Our tourist home on de la Gauchetière was located smack in the middle of Beaver Hall Hill. Everything was new and the buildings were big. My horizons were growing wider by the day.

A Fresh Start

It was a cool fall morning in November 1965 when I made my way by bus from downtown Montreal to the imposing National Film Board of Canada offices in Ville Saint-Laurent. Looking out the bus window I could see a big industrial chimney looming in the distance. We came to my stop and I was confused. Could this imposing factory along the edge of a busy highway actually be the National Film Board that was responsible for so many inventive Canadian films I had seen in Holland? In Holland, I had been making films in a converted greenhouse and town-houses. My idea of an ideal film studio was a big town house with nice gardens and manicured lawns. I was much more comfortable in a small pastoral workspace. Thinking I was in the wrong place, I asked the bus driver if we were indeed at 3155 Côte-de-Liesse. I was inclined to turn back. The driver told me to kindly get off the bus: I was at the National Film Board of Canada.

Before leaving Holland, I had sent job applications to a number of film companies in Montreal, Ottawa and Toronto. Aside from the National Film Board, or l'office national du film (NFB/ONF), the Canadian film industry was very small. People at the smaller companies I spoke to all recommended that I apply to the NFB. When I arrived at the big factory that day, I was scheduled to meet Wolf Koenig and Bob Verrall from the animation department. I had brought a 35mm show reel of my animations tucked under my arm, with some reference letters and certificates. Wolf, Bob and I had a pleasant conversation that was slightly awkward because of my limited knowledge of English. I left the reel with them, but I made up a story about needing it back for a job-hunting trip to Toronto the following Friday. When Wolf met me at the CN station that Friday to return the reel he brought a message: I should not go to Toronto, because there was an opening for me with the NFB Educational Film Unit in Montreal.

Dukke found a job as a secretary for a German company in Montreal that fabricated generators for hospitals. Her first days in Montreal were not easy, and it took a bit of adjustment to get acquainted with the city. We rented an apartment in Ville Saint-Laurent located right over a tavern. Around the corner was the Texas Galaxy Bar that attracted many men and women looking for adventure. Sometimes in the middle of the night it got pretty rowdy with fist fights on the street just below our bedroom window. This was a new experience for us, but we were young and didn't mind the noise that much. There were other places for rent in the neighbourhood, but we preferred our cosy little apartment.

At the NFB I was introduced to Jean Beaudin, a young filmmaker who was looking for an animator to help him with stop-motion projects in the French education sector: Film Scolaire. Jean had studied Art in Switzerland and was just starting to work for the NFB. We teamed up and my French improved quickly because the NFB offered French lessons and I took advantage of that. Film Scolaire was a separate unit that made films for schools on the NFB's French side. Jean and I made a number of educational films related to mathematics, such as "Dots and Lines", which connected adjacent dots to create a line.

My reel was shown to Norman McLaren and other prominent animators at the NFB who said they liked my films and encouraged me to carry on. I felt a little awkward because my work was quite different from their way of filmmaking. While their films were completely void of anything commercial, my Dutch films always had to comply with the demands of sponsors and marketing. I also worked with Robert Forget, another young and ambitious film maker who, like Jean, had studied at the University of Montreal and was new to the ONF/NFB.

One of the projects I did with Robert was called *The Skeleton/Le skelet* (1967). Robert's crew shot live-action sequences of a male athlete with a high-speed camera, and wanted to use animation to show how his skeleton moved. We did this by superimposing the animated film shots of the skeleton over the body of the athlete. In the so-called puppet studio, I built a special camera set-up to project the images of the athlete on a screen to animate the skeleton. We bought real skeletons to animate, but none of them seemed to fit. We later learned the skeletons were female. With a lot of trickery we managed to make the bones fit the body. With today's technology all this could easily be done digitally using Photoshop and After Effects.

Despite being housed in a big factory, working space in the NFB was at a premium. The big shooting stage was partitioned for a number of projects being made simultaneously.

My projects shared the big space with another film production, *Toys* (1966), an anti-war film by Grant Munro that used miniature army toys and tanks with real explosions. At the time, all the films were shot on 35mm film and later reduced to 16mm and super 8mm loops for distribution in schools. At lunch we would often go to a stuffy trailer unit next to the main building, called the Sweatbox, where we would screen cuts of films in progress. It was a great place to meet other filmmakers and see the latest films. By the mid-sixties, it had become too crowded at the ONF headquarters and we moved to a bigger office space on Paré Street near the Décarie Expressway. There was talk of opening more distribution offices and a purpose-built studio for stop motion animation, but budget constraints got in the way.

Since I was learning English and French at the same time, I ended up working on projects in both 'official' Canadian languages. I worked on some films by French Canadian filmmakers such as *Beluga Days* (1968) by Pierre Perrault, Bernard Gosselin, and Michel Brault; and I also did work for the veteran filmmaker Jacques Giraldeau. I was invited by the English Canadian producers to work on animation film projects, such as *Continental Drift* (1968), a documentary about the movements of the continents with Dr. Tuso Wilson of the University of Toronto. One day, Bob Verrall came into the studio and asked me if I would work on the project. Without hesitation, I said yes, of course. He left me with a lot of freedom. I was not accustomed to that kind of filmmaking. Unlike in Holland, there were no clients waiting, and we had total freedom to do what we wanted.

Continental Drift showed how the continents have moved apart since the beginning of Earth's history. I made the film mostly on my own in the puppet studio. A young fellow from Switzerland, Roland Stutz, helped me build and film a miniature volcano and other models for the film. We went to Toronto to film an interview with Dr. Wilson at his home in Rosedale. To demonstrate how the continents moved apart, he boiled a pot of tomato soup and we filmed the action of the moving froth on top of the boiling soup. It was my first documentary-animation film and it was well received in schools and at film festivals. Many new artists were starting to make films and it was important to find new ways to get them out to the public.

Robert Forget was one of the founders of Vidéographe, an organization to help independent video artists distribute their projects. Robert developed what he called 'The Robotheque' at the downtown NFB Montreal office. Here, films were stored on large disks and people could play them instantly without projectors from viewing stations or in a public screening room. Now we can see a film on our phone, but at the time this technology was unique in Canada. The Robotheque became an instant success, attracting thousands of visitors, including schoolchildren.

Expo 67 brought dozens of film makers from all over the world to Montreal, and to the NFB. The NFB project, prepared at the Canadair location in Ville Saint-Laurent, was a film production called *Labyrinth/Labyrinthe*, by Colin Low and Roman Kroitor (1967). The film was projected on multiple enormous screens, relating actions from one screen onto another. The Labyrinth pavilion had dimly lit walkways to guide visitors around the pavilion that made it even more mysterious. Montreal was a busy place with productions all over the place, and I was very much part of it. I would meet other filmmakers that were involved with projects for the NFB. The TP taverne in Saint-Laurent was a common place to meet.

Dukke and I got busy at home as well, and our daughter Nienke was born. I wanted to be present for the birth but I missed it all because I was still signing the hospital admission papers when she came into the world. Nienke was a delightful, pretty girl, easy to please and always smiling. A few months later, we had saved enough money to buy our first car, a brand new Renault 4. Now we had a Canadian daughter and the freedom to take her places on weekends. Having a car allowed us to travel to many places. We often went canoeing and camping in the provincial parks. La Vérendrye Wildlife Reserve was my favourite place. I particularly liked white water canoeing, and portaging past the waterfalls and rapids.

Dukke's uncle Peter, Oom Piet as we called him, had moved to Canada with a wave of Dutch immigrants in the early Fifties, and ran a farm in Ontario. When we visited him during our vacations in Grand Valley, Oom Piet showed me how to operate the tractor and other farming equipment. I helped him make hay and spread manure, and feed the animals. Little did I know that these farming experiences would come in handy later on when I became a part-time farmer. While visiting neighbouring farmers with Dukke's uncle, I also got a taste of what living was like in rural Ontario.

In 1969, two of Dukke's sisters, Hermine and Sibertha, came to visit us. Dukke was in the third trimester of her pregnancy with our second child. While visiting Terres des Hommes at the Expo site, Dukke did not feel well. She went to the site clinic where they told her the baby was about to arrive. The three sisters rushed by ambulance to the Notre Dame Hospital. By the time I arrived a nurse was carrying a baby down the stairs. Jokingly, I wondered if this was our new baby. Sure enough it was; delivery took only ten minutes, and again I missed being a witness to the birth. Anouk was a healthy, temperamental baby, with a strong voice. Hermine and Sibertha became the happy godmothers. We often would go for walks in Parc Saint-Laurent. I played a lot with my two young children before walking to work.

When the French Animation Studio got its official start with René Jodoin as its executive producer, I was already working for the French program. René started off by producing a number of films based on Quebec songwriters such as Robert Charlebois and Gilles Vigneault. By now there were many new faces at the ONF animation department: Clorinda Warney, Ron Tunis, Pierre Moretti, Pierre Hébert, Yvon Mallette, Bernard Longpré, Michèle Pauzé, Suzanne Gervais, Francine Desbiens, Lina Gagnon and many others. Together we were all part of the new French animation program.

It was here that René Jodoin encouraged me to make my first independent stop-motion film: *Oddball/Maboule.* It is a simple story about a little wire puppet who has to make a choice between little marbles and bigger balls. The puppet always prefers the bigger and more colourful balls. There is also a white ball with magic powers that the puppet ignores and rejects. At the end, he accepts the white magic ball and gives it a chance to show what it can do. At the time, I did not feel comfortable building elaborate and colourful background sets, but rather kept it very simple by using only black. I made the background completely matte by using black velvet and Polaroid filters to cut out any kind of reflections. To make the final colourful scene, I did multiple exposures using different colour filters in front of the camera lens.

Jana Bendova worked as my assistant on *Oddball/Maboule.*

Jana came from Czechoslovakia and wanted to perfect her skills as an animator, and continued helping me with other projects afterwards, like *Matrioska* (1970). *Matrioska* was a short educational film for the English animation program that demonstrated the difference between 'small' and 'big' using a set of Russian nesting dolls. The consultant on this project was Dr. Sam Rabinovitch from McGill University. Since it was an educational film, it would have no sound. After it was finished, I showed it to the NFB producers, who recommended it have music. At the Russian Embassy in Ottawa, I found Russian folk songs that I adapted to the film.

After working with me, Jana continued for many years, to work on animation films for the English animation program upstairs on the third floor. At this time another Czech, Bretislav Pojar, was at the Film Board making stop-motion films called *Balablok* (1972) and *'E'* (1981), a language parody using the letter E. Since we had similar interests, Pojar encouraged me to study puppetry in his hometown of Prague and perfect my skills as a stop-motion filmmaker. René Jodoin liked the idea, and this allowed me to go to Czechoslovakia and study in Pojar's studio and at the Faculty of Puppetry at the University of Prague. We left on a beautiful cold January morning in 1970. On the way to Czechoslovakia, I dropped Dukke and the children off in Holland to stay with her parents.

I went to visit many small towns with the puppet students from the University where they performed with string puppets at street corners and market places. These town square performances always attracted many people. I also went to visit the Jiri Trnka Studio and met other Czech filmmakers. Trnka was one of Czechoslovakia's most famous puppet filmmakers. He animated well known Czech legends, illustrated many books, and also made the highly acclaimed film, *The Hand* (1965). Due to its hidden messages about oppression, the film was banned for a while because it was too controversial.

Karel Zeman and Hermína Týrlová, two famous Czech filmmakers, stood high on the list of people I wanted to meet. Zeman explained how he made animation sequences in his studio in Gottwaldov, Moravia, to be integrated in the Jules Verne films, including the battle scenes with real horses. At the Pojar studio in Nusle they did a lot of half dimensional puppetry. Puppets were only half puppets put on a clear glass plate and animated that way. This was a style I was not familiar with. They also used paper cutouts which weren't used in Canada at the time, and their stories focused on fairy tales that spoke to children and adults.

I had a chance to do my own animation exercises. They allowed me to take some of their armature puppets and animate simple actions using the existing sets in the studio. Spending time in Czechoslovakia, now the Czech Republic, taught me many aspects of European puppet filmmaking that I still value to this day, but it was not something I wanted to copy. I preferred to explore using different materials and textiles, so I could develop my unique style of stop-motion films.

When we returned to Canada, we moved to Hudson, a small community west of Montreal, and bought a house with a large garden. We were eager to dig our hands in the soil. We walked everywhere, and had many friends in town. Behind our house was the Whitlock golf course. Sometimes the golfers hit the golf balls into our garden. We collected the stray golf balls and hit them back onto the golf course. Playing golf was not one of my favourite sports. I preferred sailing. One day when

I was out on Lac des Deux Montagnes with Paul Driessen, a sudden thunderstorm came up and blew the boat across the lake from Hudson to Oka. This was terrifying, as I had lost total control. I realized that there was nothing I could do but wait out the storm. Fortunately, the boat was fine and we sailed back. This wasn't the only time the weather got the best of me.

While I was in the middle of renovating the house and working on the leaky roof, it started to rain. I took a tarpaulin to cover part of the working space. I was nailing the tarp down when suddenly it slid down with me on top. At the edge of the roof I tried to push myself away from the wall, but I missed. I fell fifteen feet straight down into the basement entrance that was surrounded by a concrete wall. As I came crashing down, I hit my chin badly on the concrete. I literally saw stars as I came struggling up the steps, spitting out bits of teeth. Nienke was standing nearby, and when she saw me she ran inside the house calling: "Mommy, Mommy, daddy is spitting out teeth, there is blood all over, call a doctor!" Then I fainted.

An ambulance took me to the Lakeshore General Hospital. I had broken my jaw in three different places, and lost a few teeth as well. It took about four months before I could eat without a straw, and it was another half-year before my mouth was fully repaired. A friend of Dukke, Jim Clark, often came to visit and help us out in difficult times. One day he invited us for dinner. Jim did not realize that I could only have liquid food using a straw. He promptly put the steak he had prepared for supper in the blender to make it softer. It tasted awful!

While my mouth was healing, I kept thinking about the puppet work I had learned about in Czechoslovakia. Many times, I was asked about Indigenous culture in Canada. People wanted to know about the Inuit in the Far North, and assumed I must know about them. They wanted to know what the Inuit were like, how they lived and how they told their stories, but my experience in Canada was a world away from the Arctic.

My knowledge was rather limited, and I wanted to know more. Inuit culture was not something that was very well known at that time. Films on Inuit legends and mythology were almost nonexistent. At that time, the Inuit were still referred to as Eskimos, and the films I made at that time were referred to as Eskimo legends. Slowly, the word Inuit replaced the word Eskimo, but this was not common at the time. Now you only see the word Eskimo in old literature. Inuit means people. An Inuk is a person, and Inuktitut is the language spoken by the Inuit. Inuit legends have been passed down orally for centuries, long before the Europeans started to write them down. During my research, I came across many legends told by the Inuit, some that have similar versions found in the Eastern Arctic as well as in the West. It was time to start discovering the cinematic possibilities presented by the Inuit stories.

Imagining the Arctic

When you get above the treeline, the Far North is a seemingly endless space so vast that it must be experienced in person to be truly appreciated. The idea of expressing this huge expanse on film was not my intention. My real motivation was a keen interest in Inuit storytelling that I developed while studying in Europe. By 1971, the opportunity to produce imaginative films was growing fast in Canada.

I went searching for Inuit legends in the libraries at McGill University in Montreal and the Department of Northern Affairs in Ottawa, and came across a bundle of Inuit stories that were published in a magazine called *The North*. There was one story that particularly caught my attention: "The Owl and the Lemming", a tale of a hungry owl that wanted to kill and eat a lemming. In the North, the owl is seen as a rather naive and stupid creature, not the wise old owl as we know it in the South. Because of the owl's silly actions, the wily lemming escapes. It is a simple story, and seemed like a good place for me to start.

Back then, the only animated film that I knew of was based on a Tsimshian legend, a film called *The Loon's Necklace* (1948), produced by Crawley Films of Ottawa. I proposed to the producers of the ONF/NFB French animation program that I make a series of short animated films based on Inuit legends. They agreed, and I went to Iqaluit in search of local artists to collaborate with.

The first artist I met was Germaine Arnaktauyok, a young woman from the community of Igloolik. She was working at the Iqaluit artists' co-op where people did a lot of stone printing. A common object that was made for sale back then was a seal-skin owl that could be found in souvenir shops all over the country called Ookpik, the Inuit name for owl. Because Ookpik was already well-known, we decided to use the character in the film. Germaine became involved in making puppets for *The Owl and the Lemming, an Eskimo Legend/Le hibou et le lemming, une légende Eskimo* (1971). Part of her work was done in Iqaluit, but most of the production was done at the ONF in Montreal.

When Germaine first arrived in Montreal things were pretty unstable, with the separatists threatening to break up the country. The Front de libération du Québec (FLQ) had recently kidnapped the British diplomat James Cross, and killed Pierre Laporte, the Minister of Immigration, Manpower and Labour in the Quebec Government. The October crisis was still fresh on the minds of everyone, and security was tight in all public buildings. When Germaine turned up at the Montreal ONF/NFB office with her suitcase, security guards at the main entrance wanted to search it. Baffled by this request, she refused to let them look inside. There was a big argument, but at last the guards gave in and let her through. Later Germaine explained to me that she was too embarrassed to open her luggage for fear the guards would confiscate the pantyhose she had just bought at the downtown Eaton's store. She had shopped there because clothing in Montreal was a fraction of the price she paid up North.

The Inuit had to pay very high prices for any food or dry goods that did not come from the land. Most northern towns had large refrigerated cabins to store fresh fish, seal, caribou and other game for the community to freely share. The Inuit have a long tradition of sharing food and property, like dog sleds and slabs of soapstone for cooking and light. If a family was in need, the community would always share what they had. In the western world we don't always have this kind of mentality as a group, but do so individually. I was able to experience this generosity when I lived with Mina and Paulosie when I was working on *The Owl and the Raven, an Eskimo Legend/Le hibou et le corbeau, une légende Eskimo* (1973) and *Lumaaq, An Eskimo Legend/Lumaaq, une légende Eskimo* (1975). Although I compensated them for living expenses, she made me a nasaq and kamiks for free. It certainly made me feel very cared for.

Germaine got straight to work on the film. She designed the set, and cut patterns for the puppets from a large sealskin, gluing on the armatures. She prepared many of the drawings for the skies in the background of the story. I made bright, colourful panels based on these sketches, and suspended them above the set in the Montreal studio. Frame by frame I moved the panels laterally with a special device to pull the strings that were connected to the panels. This created the optical illusion of the sky moving up and down. Michèle Pauzé, one of the assistants from the French program, helped with the puppet animation and to manipulate the sky panels.

I needed a soundtrack for the film, and I met some Inuit

students from Baker Lake who had formed a music group while studying in Ottawa. They agreed to compose the songs for the film. When it was ready they proudly played me their compositions. Unfortunately, their songs were a popular style of western country music, and not appropriate for a traditional story. After a big discussion, the band leader Susan Tagoona recalled some beautiful lullabies her grandmother sang to her as a child, and she adapted them for the film.

Germaine also worked with me on the second film in the series: *The Owl and the Raven, an Eskimo Legend/Le hibou et le corbeau, une légende Eskimo*, which tells the story of how the raven became black. I was at the local CBC radio station researching traditional Inuit songs for this film when I bumped into a young Inuit woman from Iqaluit named Geela Alilkatuktuk. Geela had a baby on her back. She was at the CBC to do a talk show about how to soften sealskin. If you want to soften dried out leather, she explained in Inuktitut, you chew it with your teeth, but if your teeth are worn or if you have dentures, you have to pound it with a hammer. Geela and I chatted after her radio interview, and she became interested in doing the soundtrack for *The Owl and the Raven, an Eskimo Legend/Le hibou et le corbeau, une légende Eskimo*. We made some vague arrangements: she would need two weeks time to maybe write some songs, dialogue and narration.

When we met in Iqaluit two weeks later, Geela casually told me that everything was done: she had rewritten the story line, composed the songs, performed the voice recordings for the narration, and with the help of some relatives she had recorded all the songs. She did an amazing job. Later on, I found out that while she made the soundtrack, Geela also did her regular radio show, managed a dog kennel, fell in love and nursed a baby. How she found time to do everything at the same time is beyond me.

In the past, the Inuit women used oil lamps carved from slabs of soapstone for heat, light and cooking. The lamp was essential for survival. Another artist from Iqaluit made a beautiful miniature soapstone oil lamp that we used in *The Owl and the Raven, an Eskimo Legend/Le hibou et le corbeau, une légende Eskimo*. It had an antler drying rack for the little boots (kamiks). It was a wonderful experience to work with young Inuit artists. One young man, Alootook Ipellie from Cape Dorset, wanted to come to Montreal to learn more about animation filmmaking. He came to live at our home in Hudson while he was in the South. Alootook was very shy and withdrawn. Having a conversation with him required patience. He only nodded or shook his head, especially with strangers. To call him on the phone was the only way to get him talking.

Alootook loved to write and to draw, preferably during the night, then sleep during the day. He built the igloo for *The Owl and the Raven, an Eskimo Legend/Le hibou et le corbeau, une légende Eskimo* and animated the bone game in the story. He also performed the English narration. My children adored Alootook and were sad to see him go back to the North. Eventually, Alootook moved to Ottawa where he continued writing and drawing for the government and other publishers. But for many Northern youngsters, life in the South was difficult. Some became involved with alcohol or drugs and suffered from depression. Unfortunately, Alootook later became depressed and sadly, he died of a heart attack.

My next Inuit-inspired project was *Lumaaq, an Eskimo Legend/Lumaaq, une légende Eskimo*, a story about a jealous mother taking revenge on her son after he becomes snow-blind and can no longer hunt. I decided to do this film entirely in cut-outs that resembled stonecut prints. Every drawing on paper would be painted with black ink and then cut out. A well-known Inuit artist, Davidialuk Amituk, agreed to do the illustrations. Many of Davidialuk's drawings and sculptures have been exhibited in galleries and museums in Quebec, Ottawa and elsewhere. He loved to tell and draw stories. He only spoke Inuktitut, but with the help of his daughters we managed to communicate very well. Davidialuk was a happy old man who lived with his wife and two daughters in a crowded prefab house that looked very much like a shipping container. The washing machine and dryer stood outside because there was no room inside. The arrangement we made said that for every drawing for the storyboard he would get paid a certain amount of money. Soon I had more than enough drawings to make the storyboard for the film. Then the drawings kept coming, not just for Lumaaq but for other stories as well. Even after the flow of money stopped, beautiful drawings kept arriving at my door.

Davidialuk's drawings were cut out and placed under the camera on a glass surface with a white background underneath and replaced every second frame. The effect of the cutout drawings with their white contour lines was reminiscent of the stone prints I had seen in the northern print shops in Iqaluit. Lina Gagnon, an animation assistant, helped me and would make sure that the right cutouts were selected for the animation. Later on she assisted other animators and eventually contributed to the project Rights from the Heart/Droits au Coeur with her own film *A Family for Maria/Une famille pour Maria.* She also assisted Frédéric Back at Radio Canada for the film The Man who Planted Trees.

The Man and the Giant, an Eskimo Legend/L'homme et le géant, une légende Eskimo (1975), which tells the story of the creation of a river, became the next Inuit film in the series. I decided to combine stop-motion animation using soapstone sculptures, and live-action scenes shot out on the tundra. For the live-action shoot we decided on the location near Puvirnituq, a settlement in the eastern Arctic 1,200 kilometres north of Montreal, on Hudson Bay. Getting to Puvirnituq was a totally different experience from getting to Iqaluit. The only way to get there was, and still is, by airplane or by boat. I would fly to Val-d'Or, and then transfer to a Twin Otter to fly to Kuujjuarapik (Great Whale River), and then wait for another bush plane to fly me to Puvirnituq. These sturdy old amphibian planes were left over from WWII. Looking through little holes in the bottom of the aircraft you could see the ground or water below, and the motors were very noisy. Flight schedules depended on the weather. Now there are regular direct flights.

Puvirnituq settlement had a thriving artistic community that centred around the artists' co-op, with soapstone carving, printmaking and drama workshops. In the past, the inhabitants were mostly hunters who went fishing and seal hunting with their families on their way to the summer camps. They would also move inland to hunt for caribou. At the end of summer, they would all come back to Puvirnituq. The settlement had no theatre and no TV. Telephone was a two-way radio system that was rather awkward to use. When I was there, the Inuit gathered every Friday evening at the local mission to watch films. Often they would watch the same film over and over until a new shipment (by boat) would replace the old movies in the late spring. Most films were cowboy Wild West films with lots of horses and shooting. The young Inuit acted out thc scenes as they saw them on the screen.

The Man and the Giant, an Eskimo Legend/L'homme et le géant, une légende Eskimo took place outside at the beginning of the winter. For the live-action filming, the crew and cast travelled by canoe along Hudson Bay to our location. On the way, the Inuit would set out nets in the river to catch fish for lunch. At the film location, we put up a huge tent made from caribou skin that we attached to an overhanging rock formation. At lunchtime, the Inuit would go to the fishing nets up the river to retrieve some Arctic Char and we shared the raw fish among us. However, the cameraman and his assistant, who both came from Montreal, fashioned a table with two chairs out of the camera cases to have their canned sardines for lunch, 'white man's style'. The Inuit and I thought this was hilarious.

One fine morning when everything was ready for another live-action shoot day on location, it remained quiet in the village. Nobody showed up. The Inuit crew had all gone on strike, but no reason was given. I was told they needed time to think. Two whole weeks went by. In the meantime, I found out what was the matter: a rumour had gone around that the film would make millions of dollars on the backs of the Inuit. Therefore, they wanted more money. A meeting was called and the whole matter discussed. I made the point that this kind of filmmaking cost more money to make than it would ever earn. The films were being made for the interest of the Inuit and the general public as well as to preserve the Inuit culture and folklore. It was agreed that filming could continue.

When the cameras were ready to start rolling again, the weather turned foul. The leading actor failed to show up; he went on strike again. While canoeing to the location, one of the other actors dropped his rifle overboard. He wanted us to buy him a new rifle. By the time these problems were resolved, we had lost another precious day. Then it was argued that the filming should take place in winter with snow on the ground. But there was no snow. Again the elders had a big meeting, and they decided to go ahead with the filming anyway. Normally there should be lots of snow on the ground, but not that year. We would have to make do.

On the last day of the shooting, it started to snow ever so slightly, but it was too little too late. I learned that one of the most important aspects of good Inuit storytelling is to first determine the time of the year the story takes place. The time of the year is important because everything is related to the weather, the snow and the ice. The rest follows from that.

Paulosie Sivuak carved the soapstone sculptures for the film. They were beautiful pieces of art that depicted the story very well. I filmed the sculptures according to the storyline and animated them against neutrally coloured backgrounds. When the shooting was finished, I discovered one day that all the sculptures were missing. Someone had stolen them, or maybe the cleaners threw them out. We never found the sculptures again.

I stayed at the home of artist Paulosie and Mina Sivuak. Besides being an excellent hunter, Paulosie was also well known for his soapstone sculptures. One day, Paulosie came home with some big fat Canada geese, which Mina prepared for supper. I never got to taste the goose because they thought that I preferred only white man's food as they called it, such as canned beans, canned pork, canned sardines, canned everything. I sat at the table by myself with my canned meal while Paulosie and Mina enjoyed their food on the floor. Normally we shared our meals at the kitchen table, but when it camc to eating food from the land we always squatted on the floor

Inuit style. Luckily, I was left alone at the table only once, and the next time I happily joined them for a feast on the floor.

One day, Mina announced she would crochet a new hat for me because the one I was wearing looked rather scruffy. She quietly crocheted away until the hat (nasaq) was finished. For measurements, one look at my head was enough. Even now, during the winter some 50 years later I still wear the same nasaq, and I always get questions from Inuit I meet on the street in Montreal about where I got it.

On my way to Purvirnituq, I went camping near Kuujjuarapik in the James Bay region with university students from l'Université de Montréal. It felt good sleeping in a real warm sleeping bag. In the morning, we would start the little wood stove and wash ourselves with icy cold water from the stream beside the tent. The students were used to the harsh conditions, but I was a little reserved about it. The tundra looked magnificent with its rocks and boulders, the trees were very small and the sky was all over the place. It was like visiting another planet.

One day, I was invited to go seal hunting. It was minus 30 degrees Celsius and windy. They advised me to dress warmly because the day would be long and cold. Upon inspection, they decided that I needed two more layers of clothing. I was already wearing four layers, in fact I was wearing all the clothes I had. But at least I stayed warm. The expedition took off with five skidoos and sleds loaded with canoes and hunting gear. When we reached the ice flows, the hunters took their positions waiting for the seals to show up. After hours of waiting, we broke for lunch, which consisted of bannock, frozen fish and lots of hot tea. Then it was back to watching and waiting again. Finally, someone shouted he had spotted some seals in the distance. The excited hunters repositioned themselves to be closer to the target, but it remained very quiet.

Suddenly, there was a thundering crash. The ice started to shake and break away under our feet. "The ice is breaking, the ice is breaking," someone shouted. "Run!" We scrambled towards the edge of the ice flow. Indeed, the ice was breaking up and drifting away. We jumped to safety, but one group of Inuit were stuck on the other side trying to start their skidoo. After a seemingly endless time, the skidoo came roaring towards us, but by now the span of open water was too big to jump. Quickly they maneuvered their skidoo around to find a better spot to cross. They found a narrow gap and with a roar they forced the skidoo to jump the distance, but a sled attached to the skidoo fell into the frigid water. Finally, after lots of pushing and shouting, they managed to pull the sled out of the water and everybody was safe. By now the seal had long gone, and it was time to go back. In typical Inuit style we celebrated with fish, bannock, tea and lots of laughter. We never got the seals we were looking for, but we came home with a great story.

In 1974, the ONF/NFB invited Caroline Leaf, a well-known film animator from the U.S.A., to travel to Holman Island in the central Arctic to work with the local Inuit on the storyboard for the film *The Owl Who Married A Goose, An Eskimo Legend/Le mariage du hibou, une légende eskimo* (1974). I joined her team as technical advisor. Many changes had to be made to the story. Some Inuit ladies from Holman Island did not like the storyboard, so they rewrote the story line the way they knew it, and to make it more coherent. After working with many Inuit artists over the years, I knew how important it was to respect and involve them in telling their own stories. Caroline made the film entirely with sand animated on a light-box. It was painstaking work. The sound in the film was katajjak, or throat singing, performed by two women who face each other and start by humming the sounds. Caroline's film became popular and won a number of festival prizes.

Over the years, the Inuit have developed a thriving feature film industry. *Atanarjuat, The Fast Runner* (2001) started a new wave of successful Inuit productions such as *Uvanga* (2013). They are doing well, producing their own films now. I have fond memories of the time I spent making films of the Inuit legends. All the people I met during the time I spent up North were friendly, helpful, and most of all, generous. For me, going to the Arctic in the early Seventies began a string of events that became one of the most enriching experiences of my life.

The Very Young

When we were little kids in Holland, my father would bring home off-cuts of cloth from Opa's atelier in Amsterdam. My brothers and I would use the cloth to build tents and puppet shows, and tell our own stories using illustrations and drawings. We stamped out figures on perforated cardboard and projected the images on the walls. These experiences with my brothers and friends followed me into adulthood, and they instilled in me a life-long love of stories for children.

While I was finishing up my work on the Inuit legend films in the Arctic, I developed a new project in the South that was inspired by my own kids. One evening, Nienke and Anouk were playing in front of our fireplace with wooden construction blocks. They had drawn characters on them: one block was the mother, another the father, and others were children and animals. Holding the blocks in their little hands, the mother would go to the shopping centre to buy groceries. One child pushed a shopping cart and another pulled the dog, they were all drawn on the wooden blocks. I decided then to make a film using only wooden construction blocks with the characters drawn on the sides.

I submitted this idea to the French Program Committee and got permission to make the film, *Tchou-tchou* (1972). At that time, when you had an idea for a film project, you first discussed it with your producer. Then you got to work and put your ideas on paper. At the time I was working on *Tchou-tchou*, I worked out a rough description of my intentions and presented that to the program committee for evaluation. I also showed them samples of the artwork. It took a fair bit of convincing because some of the program committee members did not approve of the story, nor did they believe in my kind of filmmaking for children. The film is about two children and a free roaming, out of control, dragon living in a wooden block world. The boy and the girl overcome their fears of the fire-spitting dragon, and find a creative way to transform it into a tchou-tchou train.

Suzanne Gervais designed the characters and drew the basic animation on paper. All the drawings were transferred onto the wooden blocks and coloured with felt pens. The other blocks in the film were painted with coloured stains specially mixed for the film. For the animation, I had developed an innovative technique using highly polished Plexiglas cubes of different sizes that became invisible supports for the blocks as they were jumping in the air. By placing the wooden blocks on top of the Plexiglas cubes, and then turning the cubes in such a way that you could not see the sides but still look through the clear Plexiglas surface, gave the impression that the blocks were suspended in air. I had already used this method in my Russian doll film *Matrioska*, and I continued to use the Plexiglas cubes in all my other films. The carpenters at the NFB cut the blocks in different sizes, which I stained in vivid colours. To build the sets, I had a large selection of blocks to choose from. In total, there were about 2,000 blocks.

To set up each scene, I selected a number of blocks starting with the biggest ones, to compose the shots. Often there were camera movements involved. For that I would carefully build the sets around the camera, and plan the camera movements before starting the animation. One of the shots I was particularly proud of was one near the end of the film where the camera follows the train. I carefully planned some camera stops within the shot in case I had to redo a section that didn't work. For the end shot in the film, the camera follows the dragon train with the boy, the girl and the animals jumping on top of it for a ride until it ends up in the sky. I was very happy with the way it all worked out.

The finished film was well received in many festivals and public screenings. It was submitted to the Centre for Films for Children in Los Angeles where it won the Golden Star Award. I shared the award with the famous dancer Gene Kelly. The award ceremony was held at Shari Lewis's home in Hollywood. Shari was in charge of everything, including handing out the awards. She did this in a most entertaining manner, sitting at the top of the stairs with her puppet Lamb Chop. During the presentations, her shoe somehow got stuck in her gown and she came tumbling down the stairs. It all ended in a roar of laughter with a few added dance steps. *Tchou-tchou* won numerous awards that year, and is still enjoyed by children all over the world.

Most students have a curiosity that appeals to me. In the mid-seventies, I gave a workshop to a group of students from France who visited the NFB/ONF in Montreal. It was my first big workshop, and many more would follow after. I put a super 8mm camera in the middle of the room and asked the students to form a circle around it with their tables and artwork facing the camera. As they animated their creations, I moved the camera from one person to the next. By the time I came back to the first student, their next frames were ready to be shot. This way it was possible to capture their animation without losing momentum. Since then, I have given countless workshops, at festivals, during cultural events, or as a school activity (Artiste dans la Classe).

Giving animation workshops is an ideal way to teach children about movement. It is like discovering how things move and how to move things. It also teaches them about the various animation styles and techniques such as drawing animation, cut-out animation, puppet animation, stop-motion, pixilation (an animation technique animating the human body), and others. I recall working with an intellectually challenged four-year-old boy in Tilburg, The Netherlands, who animated some dried apples. With some help, the boy made his apples dance and march forward. He loved doing it, and the results were very charming.

As they grew up, my grandchildren became participants in my career. In Kingston, I would give workshops at my daughter Nienke's school where she was a teacher and where my grandson Adam was a student. Although he was shy, he expressed himself well in the workshop, and so did Tess, my granddaughter, when I went to her school. At one time, my step grandchildren, Aaron and Ariel, participated in a project where they made storyboards about Ludovic the bear and presented them at the Cinémathèque Québécoise for Les Rendez-vous du Cinéma in Montreal.

I speak three languages: English, French and Dutch. Kai, Noa and Tia, my son Nathan's children, attended a French school in Ottawa, and I conducted the workshop in French. When I gave animation workshops in Japan, Brazil, Norway, China, and other places, I always worked with a translator. Sometimes I would focus a workshop on the discovery of making things move. Other times it was about a theme, such as Christmas or the Olympics. Or a disaster such as the magnitude 7 earthquake that hit Haiti and was in the news. The kids made a story about it. When their animation was complete, we searched the Internet and found music that we could use. Laurie Gordon, my producer at the time, and the people from Les Rendez-vous du Cinéma contacted the Red Cross, who uploaded the film to YouTube to help with their fundraising campaign for earthquake relief.

The age groups for workshops varied a lot, from very young children (four to six years old) to art students, as well as the general public. In Brazil, parents also became active participants and helped their children, and some even took over. To start a typical activity, first we would sit together, discuss ideas, and prepare the artwork. To avoid complicated and messy conditions, we often would make cut-out animations on a light-box. The participants would cut or tear out shapes from coloured paper to make the characters, then place them on the light-box and start animating. With the light-box we had no issues with lights falling over, tripods hitting the camera or other accidents that often affect a stop-motion production. The images always looked very clean, and I captured the animation with a digital camera.

Over time, technology changed and the workshops changed with it. I started using super 8mm film, then later used 9-inch video disks with a Panasonic video recorder that was given to me by the research team at the Film Board. I still have all the disks stored at the NFB/ONF. Peter Foldès was invited to the NFB from France to make one of the first computer animation films: *Hunger/la faim* (1974). Peter spent a lot of time at the NRC (National Research Centre) in Ottawa to animate the film on their giant computers. It took him and the computers many months to work out all the calculations. Since Peter's landmark computer-animated film there has been an avalanche of CGI films along with a series of executive producers to leave their signatures on the French Animation studio after René Jodoin: Pierre Moretti, Yves Leduc, Robert Forget, Marcel Jean, Pierre Hébert and René Chénier.

At this time, the English program asked me to work on a feature film called *Running Time* (1974), by Mort Ransen. The animator Ryan Larkin and I worked together to do the animation sequences for the film, and experimented a lot with the actors running against animated backgrounds. We applied very rudimentary special effects to make the actors run or fly in the sky. First, we would film the actors in stop-motion running on the spot, and then superimpose the animated backgrounds. One sequence that I was particularly proud of was the canoeing song with all the letters coming out of the mouths of the performers. I projected each frame of the singers on the animation stand, timed the words very carefully, and placed the cut-out letters on the precise spot on the background. The letters were all individually animated, white on black. I did it all in one shot.

I was asked to do the camera work and visual effects for a semi-animated experimental film called *Monsieur Pointu* (1975), by André Leduc and Bernard Longpré. I found it fun and challenging. Since the action had to be shot against a black background, the camera lens and studio lights had to be polarized. To manipulate the violins, hats and ribbons on camera, assistants wore special black masks and clothing to make themselves invisible. Among many accolades, the film received an Academy Award nomination.

While I was making all these projects for children, I had a strong desire to have another child with Dukke. She was quite opposed to that idea because being pregnant was too much trouble, and having to change diapers again was not very appealing. "What about adopting a child?" she suggested. I liked the idea a lot, and soon after we set the process in motion. We went to the Catholic Children's Services in Montreal for interviews. There we met Nathan, a young boy with a difficult start in life, but he seemed healthy, in good spirits, and energetic.

We brought three-year-old Nathan home, and six months later we officially adopted him into our family. His father was African American and his mother was Polish, that was all we knew of his background. At first, the girls were a little apprehensive about him, but it did not take long for them to come around. Nathan loved cars. He had a red toy car that he drove around the living room. That was his special toy, but we had to get rid of the car because it was too dangerous with the sharp edges sticking out.

Nathan was an active boy who loved cars and played drums. He still loves cars, and he plays drums in a band called "The Start". Playing soccer was his favourite sport growing up, but because of knee injuries he had to give it up. Nathan studied at the police academy in Nicolet, Quebec. When he graduated, he was immediately hired by the police force in Ottawa. He worked his way up to become a detective, but eventually left to become the manager of security for local housing projects in Ottawa. I am proud to have Nathan as my son.

As our family grew, we decided we wanted to have more space around us. Hudson was too suburban for Dukke; she wanted to be closer to nature. At that time, the political climate in Quebec was pretty volatile, so we cruised the country roads just across the provincial border in Ontario. One day, a farmer told me that there was a place for sale in Dalhousie Mills, right on the border with Ontario. In fact, a small corner of the land is in Quebec. We drove up to the farm and met the farmer, who indeed wanted to sell his 100-acre farm privately. He was in his eighties and had just retired.

Everything went very fast and I found the whole thing quite overwhelming. Before we knew it, we became the new owners. I had to learn many new skills to farm part-time. I followed courses in agriculture and land management at MacDonald College in Sainte-Anne-de-Bellevue and learned from neighbouring farmers how to work the fields. We did not need to buy any farm equipment, as it was included when we bought the farm. Soon we got our first animals: a goat, then a Jersey cow, followed by Snorky the pig, and two horses.

The kids took the school bus to the next village in Glen Robertson for school. Farm life was very different. When you wake up, the animals have to be fed and the stalls need to be cleaned, but the children liked the animals in their care. Anouk had a little duckling that followed her all over the yard. The two were inseparable. She also had another duckling with a third leg on top of her head, which fortunately, did not live long. Dukke did not work away from the farm. She was very busy with the farm animals and the kids.

In the middle of the field stood a small maple grove with a collapsed maple syrup shack. I renovated the sugar cabin and every year I would make maple syrup, mostly for our own consumption. Living on the farm became more demanding as time went on. In addition to the big animals, we had even more goats, sheep, pigs, rabbits, geese and chickens. We planted thousands of trees and renovated the house as best we could. The stable was completely rebuilt. To top it all off, I had some beehives as well. Every year I would extract and sell the honey, along with eggs and butter to friends, and film board colleagues. I loved making maple syrup, planting trees and beekeeping.

It was too far to commute to Montreal every day, so I made arrangements to work four 10-hour days per week. Midweek I stayed at home, the other days I stayed with friends or slept in my office. At that time, there were other filmmakers who slept in their offices at the Film Board and sometimes I would bump into them. It was hard work dividing my time between farming and filmmaking. But being left on my own in the studio for days at a time proved useful. I was now ready to embark on my most ambitious film, which would deliver me one of the biggest moments of my film career.

The Sand Castle

Who knows which project will stand out from the others in a career? Life is fickle. When you embark on a project you are certain it will be the best thing ever, but it doesn't always work out that way. Other times, you can do something very special and it fails to find an audience for reasons that are a mystery.

In the late seventies, I had the good fortune to work on a project that, I believe, was a creative success as well as a critical success. My perfect film was *The Sand Castle/Le château de sable* (1977). Again, my children inspired me. As part of our summer vacation, we rented a cottage on the island of Vlieland, in the northern part of Holland. Every day we would go to the beach, and Nienke, Nathan and Anouk would build a magnificent castle surrounded by high walls and canals. Every night the tide would rise and wash it all away. But the next day the kids came back and happily started all over again. The joy was in the building.

Watching my kids play in the sand, I developed the idea of imaginary sand creatures who build a castle to protect themselves. When I brought this idea to the NFB's program committee, they again gave me a bit of trouble. Some members argued strongly against the idea, and others were just lukewarm. When I was invited to defend my film, the committee members were again divided in their opinions. Most members were documentary filmmakers who had no idea what animation was all about. I was rather nervous to do my presentation and it did some convincing to win them over. Few were in favour, but others had a hard time with the project. I must say that sometimes a film project needs to be presented multiple times before it is accepted. So far, I had been lucky. In the end, the project was accepted and I would happily play with sand for the next year or so.

First, I needed some sand. On the way home from work, I drove past some sandy looking hills. I stopped the car and climbed over a fence to fill up some bags. Just then, someone came out of the house on his way to a barn with two dogs. I grabbed my sandbags and left the barking dogs behind as fast as I could. At the studio I filtered the sand for dirt, separating it into boxes with lighter and darker colours and textures.

Traditionally, animators would make latex, rubber or silicone moulds to create their puppets. But I decided to go a different route. I took a large foam rubber mattress and with a pair of scissors cut slabs of foam rubber and sculpted each character for the film. Then I cut a hole inside the puppets to insert wire armatures and submerged the puppets in liquid latex to give them more integrity. Then I covered the puppets with sand and cured them in the oven for a couple of hours at 150 degrees. Some puppets collapsed while being baked and had to be redone.

One morning, I walked into my office and sensed something

Left to right: Ferry, Jos, Co. Amsterdam, 1942.

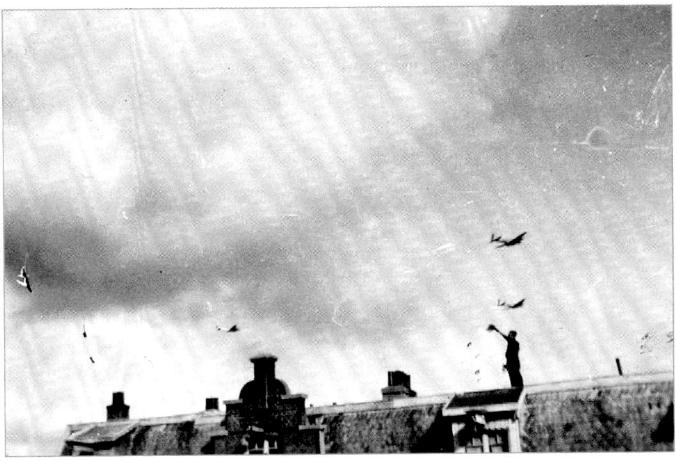

Papa standing on the roof. Liberation of Amsterdam, 1945.

Co and Ferry. Amsterdam, 1949.

Family portrait, Left to right: Sitting on floor – Ria . Second row – Ans, Mama, Frans. Third row – Ferry, Co, Jos. Back row – Papa. Amsterdam, 1950.

Co shooting with a Parvol L camera at Cinecentrum, Hilversum, 1959.

Two soldiers serving Sergeant Co. Alexander Kazerne, The Hague, 1961.

Nevada wool commercial. Cinecentrum, Hilversum, 1963.

Co and Dukke van der Werf waving goodbye (far left). Rijndam, Rotterdam, 1965.

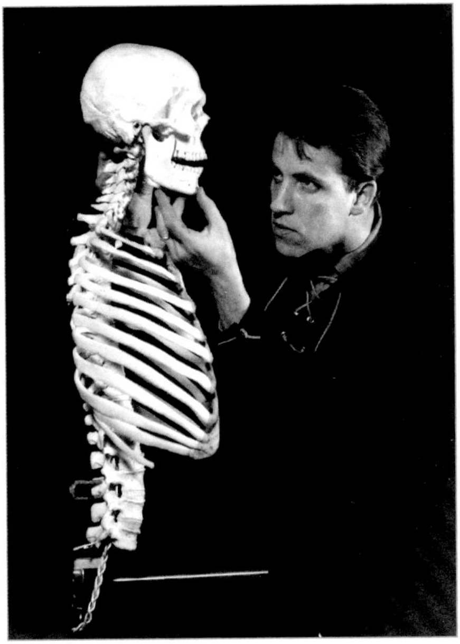

Co animating the skeleton, a film directed by Robert Forget. *The Skeleton/le skelet*, © National Film Board of Canada, 1967.

Co and Roland Stutz filming volcano model. *Continental Drift/La dérive des continents*, © National Film Board of Canada, 1968.

Oddball/Maboule, © National Film Board of Canada, 1969.

Matrioska, © National Film Board of Canada, 1970.

Co writing script, Iqaluit, Baffin Island. *The Owl and the Lemming: An Eskimo Legend/Le hibou et le lemming: une légende eskimo*, © National Film Board of Canada, 1971.

Germaine Arnaktauyok working on the puppets. *The Owl and the Lemming: An Eskimo Legend/Le hibou et le lemming: une légende eskimo*, © National Film Board of Canada, 1971.

Puppets made by Germaine Arnaktauyok. *The Owl and the Raven: An Eskimo Legend/Le hibou et le corbeau: une légende eskimo*, © National Film Board of Canada, 1973.

Lumaaq drawing by Davidialuk Amituk. *Lumaaq: An Eskimo Legend/Lumaaq: une légende eskimo*, © National Film Board of Canada, 1974.

Lumaaq drawing by Davidialuk Amituk. *Lumaaq: An Eskimo Legend/Lumaaq: une légende eskimo*, © National Film Board of Canada, 1974.

Sculpture by Paulosie Sivuak. *The Man and The Giant: an Eskimo Legend/L'homme et le géant: une légende eskimo*, © National Film Board of Canada, 1975.

Tchou-tchou, © National Film Board of Canada, 1972.

Tchou-tchou, © National Film Board of Canada, 1972.

Left to right: Dukke van der Werf, Anouk Hoedeman, Mama van der Werf, Nienke Hoedeman, Nathan Hoedeman. Hudson, Quebec, around 1972.

Left to right, back row: Nienke Hoedeman, Co, Dukke van der Werf. Front row: Anouk Hoedeman, Cognac, Nathan Hoedeman, Princesse. Family photo at the farm, 1976. Photo by Nico Crama.

Camera setup. *The Sand Castle/Le château de sable*, © National Film Board of Canada, 1977.

Co animating. *The Sand Castle/Le château de sable*, © National Film Board of Canada, 1977.

The Sand Castle/Le château de sable, © National Film Board of Canada, 1977.

Co and Paul Driessen after they were jointly awarded the Grand Prix at the Annecy film festival in 1977. Photo by Nico Crama.

Co with his Oscar® for Best Short Film, Animated, ©A.M.P.A.S.® 1977.

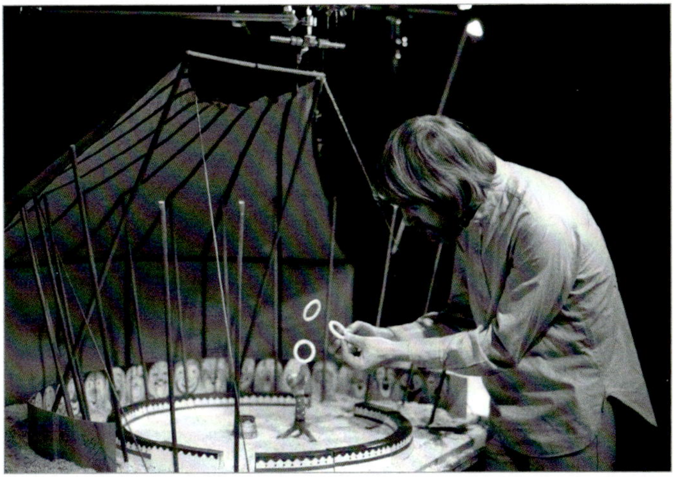

Co animating discs for the film *Co Hoedeman, Animator/Co Hoedeman, animateur*. A co-production with Nederlands Omroep Stichting, directed by Nico Crama. © National Film Board of Canada, 1980.

Treasure of the Grotoceans/Le Trésor des Grotocéans, © National Film Board of Canada. 1980.

Co setting up a shot. *Mascarade*, © National Film Board of Canada, 1984.

Co in the set. *Charles and François/Charles et François*, © National Film Board of Canada, 1987.

Charles and François/Charles et François, © National Film Board of Canada, 1987.

Charles and François/Charles et François, © National Film Board of Canada, 1987.

The Box/La boîte, © National Film Board of Canada, 1989.

On the set. *The Box/La boîte*, © National Film Board of Canada, 1989.

The Sniffing Bear/L'ours renifleur, © National Film Board of Canada, 1992.

The Sniffing Bear/L'ours renifleur, © National Film Board of Canada, 1992.

Camera setup. *The Garden of Ecos/Le jardin d'Écos*, © National Film Board of Canada, 1997.

Ecos and her baby. *The Garden of Ecos/Le jardin d'Écos*, © National Film Board of Canada, 1997.

Co animating the paper puppet. *The Garden of Ecos/Le jardin d'Écos*, © National Film Board of Canada, 1997.

On the set. *The Garden of Ecos/Le jardin d'Écos*, © National Film Board of Canada, 1997.

Camera set up. *Ludovic, The Snow Gift/Ludovic - Une poupée dans la neige*, © National Film Board of Canada, 1998.

Ludovic, The Snow Gift/Ludovic – Une poupée dans la neige, © National Film Board of Canada, 1998.

Ludovic, A Crocodile in my Garden/Ludovic – Un crocodile dans mon jardin,
© National Film Board of Canada, 2000.

NFB Float Santa Claus Parade Left to right: Front row: Aaron Blair, Ariel Blair. Second row: Co, Jessica Blair, Tess McIsaac, Adam McIsaac, Ludovic puppet. Third row: Julie Roy NFB producer French program, parade staff, puppeteer from Théâtre sans fils. Photo by Joyce Ryckman.

Left to right: Jessica Blair, Ariel Blair, Joyce Ryckman, Co, Aaron Blair. New Year's Eve 2000.

Anouk's wedding. Left to right, back row: Jessica Blair, Joyce Ryckman, Co, Dukke van der Werf, Anouk Hoedeman, Alex deVries, Nathan Hoedeman, Mary McLean, Nienke Hoedeman. Front row: Kai Hoedeman, Ariel Blair, Aaron Blair, Adam McIssac, Noa Hoedeman, Tia Hoedeman, Tess McIssac.

In Kihachirō Kawamoto's studio. Left to right: Koji Yamamura, Co, Sumire, Kihachirō Kawamoto, 2000.

Women carrying Shad. *Winter Days*, directed by Kihachirō Kawamoto, 2003.

Marianne's Theatre/Le théâtre de Marianne, © National Film Board of Canada, 2004.

Co setting up puppets. *Marianne's Theatre/Le théâtre de Marianne*, © National Film Board of Canada, 2004.

Co working with students at the Queensland Art Gallery, Australia, 2004.

Handmade paper awards designed and made by Co Hoedeman for the Ottawa Animation Festival, 1992.

WWII, Holland. *55 Socks/55 Chaussettes/55 Sokken*, © National Film Board of Canada, 2011.

People searching for food. *55 Socks/55 Chaussettes/55 Sokken*, © National Film Board of Canada, 2011.

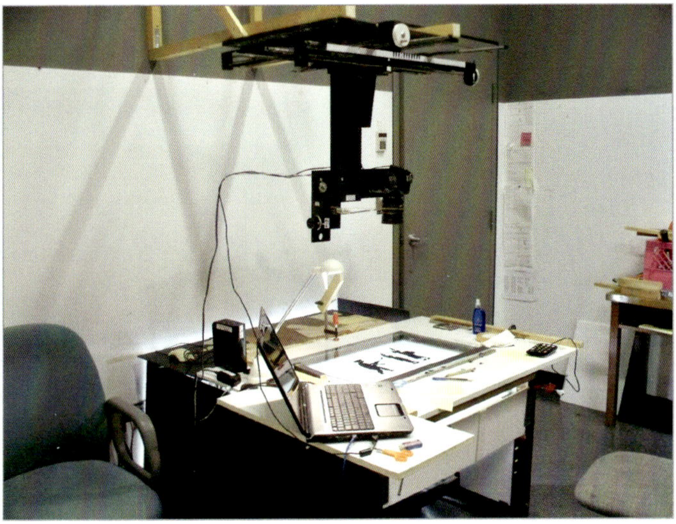

Camera set up at NFB. *The Blue Marble/La bille bleue*, 2014.

Cranes with instructions for digitization. *The Blue Marble/ La bille bleue*, 2014.

Co in front of some of his artwork at The Musée de la civilisation in Quebec City, 2014. Photo by Jessica Blair.

Close up of display. *Charles and François/Charles et François*, 1987, © National Film Board of Canada, The Musée de la civilisation in Quebec City, 2014. Photo by Jessica Blair.

Cardinal alighting on branch. *The Cardinal/Le cardinal*, 2016.

Girl watching the cardinal. *The Cardinal/Le cardinal*, 2016.

Co's 81st birthday. Left to right: Nathan Hoedeman, Jessica Blair, Co, Alex deVries, Anouk Hoedeman, Nienke Hoedeman. Photo by Joyce Ryckman, 2021.

Co and Joyce on the promenade deck in Quebec City for the Fête National. Timeless. Photo by Janice Johnson.

was not right. Some of the puppets were missing. Indeed, half of them were gone. Somebody had taken The Sand Castle puppets! The stolen puppets were never recovered. So I started over. On another occasion, a stray cat managed to get into the studio, and during the night used the film set as a litter box. Unavoidably, the shot I was working on was ruined, and had to be redone.

During the time I made *The Sand Castle/Le château de sable*, tools like video assist, already in use in the U.S., and motion control, did not exist at the NFB. Everything was still done manually, and the only way to see an image was by looking through the camera's viewfinder. One morning while shooting a scene I had spent two days setting up, I decided to go for a cup of coffee. When I got back to my studio, there was a delegation of Japanese visitors admiring the film set. I wondered where the visitors had found the puppets they were passing around, until I realized that they had lifted them straight out of the scene I was shooting. The shot was ruined and had to be completely redone.

While building the sand creatures and the castle, I had to keep the sand moist but I could not use water, because it would dry out and the structures would collapse. Instead, I mixed glycerine with the sand, which appeared wet for days and also kept my skin nice and soft. In the studio there was sand everywhere; it even managed to get inside the camera. While setting up a shot to film the sandstorm, I heard some grinding noises coming from the camera. The aperture of the lens got stuck and would not move. Tiny grains of sand had gotten inside the lens. It was ruined.

Things got off to a rocky start when I went to submit the finished film to the Annecy International Animation Film Festival. We were already late submitting the film, and the sound track was still separate from the film (double track). At first, festival officials refused to accept the film. After a big spat between the festival and the NFB officials, the selection committee allowed the film to be entered in competition. When the film was shown, it received a roaring applause. *The Sand Castle/Le château de sable* was awarded the Grand Prix ex aequo, along with the film *David* (1977) by my Dutch compatriot and friend Paul Driessen.

Riding this early success, the film was entered into several other festivals and submitted to the Academy of Motion Picture Arts and Sciences in Hollywood. Two NFB films received Oscar nominations that year in the short animated film category: mine and *The Bead Game/Histoire de perles* (1977), by my friend Ishu Patel. During the lead up to the Oscars, Hollywood was a beehive of activities, and although I felt a little lost amongst the stars, I felt triumphant when The Sand Castle took the honour. This was the first Oscar for the NFB/ONF since Norman McLaren won with *Neighbours/Voisins* (1952).

Jodie Foster and Paul Williams handed me the Oscar for best animated short at the ceremony in early 1978. In my acceptance speech, I thanked the Academy and particularly the NFB/ONF for supporting the many filmmakers and giving us the opportunity to express ourselves freely. Because I was tense and nervous, I totally forgot to thank Dukke and the kids. After my little speech, Jodie Foster and I walked off stage together to the pressroom. In an effort to get a conversation going I naively asked Jodie if she was also involved in filmmaking. Her answer was simple: "You bet I am." And that was the end of our conversation.

In the pressroom, the media didn't ask me anything, or take

any pictures. It was a weird feeling, as if I was not part of the show. The night I received the Oscar, Beverly Shaffer, also from the NFB, won an Oscar for her live-action short *I'll Find A Way/ Je trouverai un moyen* (1977). It was unheard of that the NFB/ ONF would win two Oscars in one night. While the after-party was still going on, we stored both Oscars in a locker for safety and went back to the party, dancing our way late into the night.

The following morning at the Beverly Hilton Hotel, the driver of a large yellow school bus announced the last call to go to the airport. I was eager to go home. Quickly I got my luggage, wrapped the Oscar inside a newspaper and got onto the bus. The driver was complaining bitterly about all the commotion, and said he would be happy when the fuss was all over. "There are limousines all over the place blocking the streets," he complained to me, his only passenger on the bus. I mentioned that I was an Oscar winner for *The Sand Castle/Le château de sable*. He could not believe it and wanted to know everything about winning the Academy Award. I unwrapped my trophy and showed him the statuette. When I told him what happened the night before at the Oscars, his day was made. He would share the experience with his family. He closed the doors of the bus, and without delay or any other stops raced me to the airport through L A. traffic.

At the Air Canada counter, the ticket agents promised to upgrade my seat, but they were so busy admiring the Oscar they forgot all about it. As the plane came in for a landing in Montreal, the co-pilot announced on the intercom that there was an Oscar winner on board, and there may be some delay in de-boarding the plane. A local CBC news crew was waiting for me at the gate to do an interview. A small group of animators and friends greeted me at the airport as well. Back at home everyone was excited, especially the kids.

A short while later, I called my parents in Holland to tell them about the Oscar. In the Netherlands, the Academy Awards were not as well known as in Canada, and they had no idea what I was referring to. At first they thought I had a new dog called Oscar. When I told them it was a big award they were duly impressed and delighted. The Oscar brought the film a lot of exposure that included me doing many interviews and travelling to different places. Unfortunately, it took me away from my studio for about three months.

After *The Sand Castle/Le château de sable*, I made the film *The Treasure of the Grotoceans/Le Trésor des Grotocéans* (1980) dealing with values and treasures. It fascinates me to see how things change in value. When there is a shortage of materials the value rises. The contrary is true as well. This film also received some awards for its innovations and creativity, but not nearly as many as *The Sand Castle/Le château de sable*. Like the puppets from *The Sand Castle/Le château de sable*, the characters in this film were also cut from slabs of foam rubber, painted with coloured ink and cured in the oven.

For the underwater scenes, I used mainly invisible wire to suspend the characters when swinging in the air or swimming underwater. The underwater effects were created by putting a clear, distorted Plexiglas disk in front of the lens. Turning the disc frame by frame created the underwater undulations. Because the disk was not overly clear, it helped me to obscure the threads and wires suspending the puppets.

I believe the NFB has won 11 Oscars over the years. One day, someone wanted to show off all the Oscars in Ottawa as part of a big showcase. A number of the statuettes were sent for the occasion, including mine. Months later a package containing the Oscars came back. They were all wrapped together roughly, and taped together with scotch tape. Trying to peel the tape off caused the gold leaf to come off the statuettes and the damaged Oscars had to be sent back to Hollywood for repairs. Even though they were expensive to repair, the Academy never complained about the damage.

After winning the Oscar, those who had been opposed to my ideas in the past became more open to them. Years later, one of the NFB's committee members, Werner Nold, an editor at the NFB, who was initially opposed to *The Sand Castle/ Le château de sable* concept, apologized for doubting it, and offered high praise for the finished film. We were good friends, and later we worked together on some of my films.

Recognition for my work mostly came from outside the country at that time. The Oscar led to world recognition, and with it came invitations to give workshops and teachings about animation, mainly to children, but also to adults. Later, I was invited to give Master Classes in animation. Giving Master Classes is very rewarding. The participants always have many questions particularly about the making of my films. Where do I get inspiration? Do I work with a large team or all by myself? My answers are always the same. Children inspire me a lot, and I work mostly by myself with some assistance. It is nice to be recognized by your colleagues and friends. It gives you satisfaction and the desire to carry on. Receiving awards is a big part of it that is very stimulating. It gives you the feeling of being on the right track.

Big Changes

Despite my earlier ambivalence about industry awards, winning the Oscar for *The Sand Castle/Le château de sable* changed my career in a very positive way. It brought exposure to my work, as well as an interest in how I lived my life in Canada. To the Dutch, being both a farmer and a filmmaker was unusual. Dutch film producer Nico Crama was commissioned by NOS, a TV station in The Netherlands, to make a documentary film about how I managed to accomplish my studio work while living on the farm with my family. The NFB came on board as co-producer of the documentary titled *Co Hoedeman, Animator/Co Hoedeman, Animateur* (1980).

To provide action for the studio portion of the film I made a new character called Snuffle, a little three-legged foam rubber puppet. Stop-motion acrobatics by Snuffle were set in a miniature circus tent. Snuffle performed jumps and somersaults, and dove through hoops and rolled like a ball on the platforms before recovering into his original shape. On the farm, Nico filmed us horseback riding, milking cows, making butter and cheese, driving the tractor, plowing the fields and making hay. During filming, Nico and I developed a lasting friendship. Later, whenever I visited Holland, I would always drop in for coffee at his home in Scheveningen.

When the film was shown on TV, it did very well. People were intrigued by the fact that I could make films and continue to farm. Once, when I showed *The Sand Castle/Le château de sable* at a family reunion in Holland, the adults were fascinated by it all, but the younger generation were restless and made sarcastic comments and jokes about the film. They were not at all interested in watching it. This is the only time that has happened.

The next film I made was *Mascarade*, a half hour television show about creativity. It was inspired by my daughter Anouk, who had made a cardboard robot that she wore at a school presentation. The sets for the film were pretty elaborate and we made many accessories for the different scenes. Nina May helped me as an animation assistant in the studio. Francine Gagné and Lilian Kruip prepared the sets and made costumes for the puppets. Jean Charlebois wrote the text for the songs in the film. I think it is a pretty good effort, but it missed the mark, and the finished film was not overly popular.

However, I did not consider it a failure. It was my first attempt to make a film for television, and my last until the *Ludovic* television series. I recall another time when I totally missed the mark. Together with Roch Carrier, who wrote the story of *The Sweater/Le chandail* (1980), we explored the idea of combining live-action puppetry with stop-motion animation. Roch and I would meet regularly to work out ideas, but sometimes we would clash if it did not work out. In the end, we had a story outline that we presented to the program committee. Our ideas were not worked out very well, and the program committee refused it. That was the only time any of my projects were refused. Actually, I was glad that they did not like it, because I was not ready for this kind of adventure. The whole story was too complicated.

In 1988, I was invited to be a jury member for the first international animation film festival in Shanghai, China. It was an event that took place in the middle of winter. Everything was pretty lavish with many performances, receptions and terrific Chinese food. After the festival, I was invited to stay on at the Shanghai Animation Studio for four more weeks. I stayed in the same room where Kihachirō Kawamoto made the film *To Shoot Without Shooting* (1988). The students taught me to play Mahjong. We often met in my room to play the game because it was cold in the buildings, and I had the good fortune to have heating in my room. However, the water heater in the bathroom did not work. To wash and dry myself, I put my damp towel over the radiator to heat it up and then drape it over my shivering body.

I borrowed someone's bicycle that gave me freedom to sightsee. The streets were always crowded with cyclists. At one time, the bicycle traffic was so heavy coming in the opposite direction that it took me 10 minutes to make a left turn. Finally, there was a break in the traffic and all the cyclists together dashed across. I was not the only one who needed to go that way. If I wanted to visit other cities I had to get special permission, because the Mao dictatorship was still in power. One time, I was allowed to visit a puppet theatre group in Shaanxi in the province of Xian. They did a shadow puppet performance with the images projected on a big white sheet. From time to time I could see the puppeteers projected on the screen, and that made it even more special. It was all in Chinese, and my translator did her best to help me understand the play, but that did not work. Despite the language barrier, it was not hard to figure out that the theatre group, who were responsible for my expenses, had very little money. Everything was very simple and basic, but I didn't mind at all because there was no lack of kindness. In the morning, before my Chinese breakfast of rice porridge, dumplings, tofu and tea, the water ladies were constantly pouring hot water in the bathtubs for us to wash ourselves. I could also go to the communal bathhouse to shower, which I did, and as I was the only European among the Chinese they all stopped what they were doing to watch me shower.

I managed to get permission to travel to Xian to see the unearthed soldiers of the Terra Cotta Army. Most impressive indeed. The site was closed to the public, but me and my friend from the puppet theatre were allowed in as long as we did not take any photographs. I was struck by the individuality of the Terra Cotta Soldiers, the expressions on their faces, the horses and chariots as well. Secretly, I photographed some of the sculptures.

From Shaanxi, I travelled to the coastal city of Dalian. There I was invited to give a lecture on animation followed by a presentation of my films. At the new animation studio they were building, there was a lot of construction going on, so the place was half finished. When I tried to show my films to the students there was no electricity in the room, so we ran an extension cord from two floors below to power the projector. That did not last long. The circuit overloaded when the construction workers turned on their power tools. Now the whole building was plunged into darkness, and sadly, the students never got to see my films.

Back in Canada, I became intrigued with the relationship children have with their grandparents and what happens when you age, particularly when you become a centenarian. What if ageing could be slowed down for one and sped up for another? In film everything is possible. I worked on the film *Charles and François/Charles et François* (1987) with Jean Charlebois, who developed the story into a moving and dramatic script where a grandfather and his grandson are both 100 years old at the same moment. One chooses to end his life and the other decides to live on. *Charles and François/Charles et François* is my most complex film, and my personal favourite.

Again, I combined animated drawings with cut-outs and stop-motion animation. All the characters were first drawn on paper by Stefan Anastasiu, then transferred and glued onto cardboard and cut out. These cut-out shapes were placed in the set and animated like stop-motion characters. I found the results fascinating, and I realized that I could combine any type of animation technique to tell a story. Sometimes I would visit François Dompierre in his studio in Saint-Bruno to listen to the film's music composition in progress and suggest changes if needed. *Charles and François/Charles et François* did very well on the festival circuit.

Over the years, I have had several assistants helping me with the animation in the studio. Nina May had helped me on the film *Mascarade*, and was now assisting me on *Charles and François/Charles et François*. She had just finished communication studies at Concordia University in Montreal. A few years later, for *The Garden of Ecos/Le jardin d'Écos* (1997), Nina was hired again to do the computer effects. She was very pleasant to work with and became a good friend. Chantal Roy worked with me on two productions: *Charles and François* and *The Box/La boîte* (1989). She was particularly good at preparing the artwork. It is important for an artist to have people around them who support their work and their ideas, and be able to contribute to the development of the work.

Unfortunately during this time, I was in the middle of a divorce process with Dukke. We had drifted apart, Dukke had her own priorities and interests and I had mine. We just didn't get along anymore and I believed that she did not support my work. Divorce had a profound effect on me. Even though it was my decision, I was struggling a lot. Not only did I end the relationship, my whole lifestyle had to change. After I separated from Dukke, I moved away from the farm and lived on my own in an apartment in Montreal. That alone made it very hard.

Luckily, I was surrounded by many friends. I mostly focused on my work. In my spare time, I played volleyball with friends. Many times I felt pretty lonely. Not having to do the farm work and caring for the animals or working the fields made it sometimes very difficult. On the other hand, it gave me the freedom to travel and hang out with my city friends. I indulged myself in exploring different art forms, which I enjoyed very much. Living in the city opened new possibilities.

Sometimes I miss the carefree country living and being close to the earth, but after all, it was the right decision to move away from the farm. The children were grown up and on their own, except for Anouk. She was still in high school and living at home. Soon after she graduated, she went to The Netherlands to stay with family and found a job in a department store. She also improved her Dutch language skills. At first, living back in Montreal was exciting, but often I would feel very lonely. I missed the tranquility of the country.

The Next Chapter

As a child, my brothers and I would use discarded shoeboxes and transform them into mini theatres, or peep shows (kijkdozen). A hole was cut in the front of the box to be used to peek inside. We would then draw illustrations of typical fairy tales such as *Hansel and Gretel*, and *Cinderella*. The illustrations were neatly cut out, glued on a roll of paper and placed in the back of the box. The cover of the box was cut open and re-covered with coloured transparent paper. Pulling the drawings from side to side in the back of the box, I would tell the story. Other kids in the neighbourhood also made these shoebox peep shows. The smart ones would ask five cents per viewing, or three peeks for a dime.

For *The Box/La boîte*, I expanded on my childhood peep show experience, combining stop-motion animation, pixilation and live-action shooting. Some live-action sequences I performed on my own, and for others I animated myself frame by frame, like pixilation. For the artwork, I drew the characters on thin cardboard and cut them out precisely. They had to stand up on their own in the set. Whenever the characters moved, I would exchange their cut-outs for other cut-out shapes and put them back in the set. Chantal Roy helped me with the preparations.

First, I wrote the outline of the story, then I put it into the storyboard, which is the story in pictures. It was up to me to take it from there and work it all out on the set in front of the camera. All my actions were worked out beforehand, there was no one to guide me. Often I would use my free hand to guide the action. I fully concentrated on the action at hand from start to finish. For the next shot, it would start all over again. Sometimes I had to do the shot another time if the action was not to my satisfaction.

In the winter of 1989, I met Joyce Ryckman, the woman who would become my second wife. My friend, Doris May, invited me to her vernissage at the Montreal Botanical Garden. Walking in from the cold I noticed this beautiful woman standing in the doorway to the exhibition talking to Doris. I went over to introduce myself. Joyce was wearing a fur-trimmed hat that looked very soft and I began touching it. Needless to say she was somewhat surprised, but laughed about it. Soon after, we started dating and fell in love. It all happened very fast. We met and never parted. Once, someone asked me why I came to Canada, "To meet Joyce", I said.

Joyce is an artist and writer. She was able to help me with the ending of *The Box/La boîte*, suggesting that the little boy send the star to its rightful place in the universe instead of being tacked to a wall. She gave me valuable advice and continued to be the artistic adviser on all my films from then on. Meeting Joyce brought an end to my bachelor days. Each time I visited Joyce, I took some of my furniture and fit it into her apartment. My lease was up and I had other plans than renewing it. When I finally moved in it seemed as if I had run and won a marathon.

It was the beginning of a new and enduring chapter in my life.

When I first met Joyce, my children were adults and on their own, and Joyce had a 14 year old daughter, Jessica. I was now going to have two families. At the age of eight, Jessica was stricken with encephalitis that left her with memory loss and uncontrolled epilepsy. The side-effects of one of her medications in particular made her life quite difficult. However, despite this, she is a very good photographer and exhibits her work.

When I was invited to go to Venezuela, I wanted Joyce to come along. She has a fear of flying, so it took a lot of convincing to get her to agree. I was in Cleveland giving film presentations, so we agreed to meet in New York and fly to Venezuela together from there. When I met Joyce at LaGuardia Airport she was quite anxious. The flight to Venezuela was calm and peaceful. Caracas is a beautiful city surrounded by several mountains. There is a lot of poverty, and many people live in little makeshift houses located on the hills surrounding the city.

After my film presentations at Simón Bolívar University in Caracas, we flew to Mérida in the Andes where we were invited by the Alliance Française for me to give lectures and film presentations, and for Joyce to give a talk on her art. The Mérida landing strip is located between two mountains and is very short. Our translator, Pedro, jokingly said that the landing instructions from the air controller to the pilot were Hail Mary's. It all went very well, but I still have Joyce's finger prints on my arm.

At that time, there was a lot of tension between the police and the students. Every day there were riots in the streets; one day, an Argentinian foreign student was hauled off a bus and shot by the police. At the Alliance Française when Joyce was in the middle of her presentation the riots moved in too close for comfort. Tear gas filled the building and it was too dangerous to continue. We were taken to one of the official's houses and treated to some very delicious Venezuelan food. In the evening, the lectures and film presentations continued at the Alliance Française as if nothing had happened earlier. It was all a bit surreal.

When we were in Caracas, the cultural attaché at the Canadian Embassy asked Joyce what she would like to do in Merida. She said that she would like to meet the folk artists whose work she had seen in numerous books at the university. A reception was organized at the museum, but because of the riots we could not get there. Needless to say we were extremely disappointed, especially when we later learned that many of the artists had made the dangerous trip from the mountains to meet us at the museum.

On a day off, we hired a taxi for a trip into the Andes. The driver of the old beaten-up taxi took us up the steep roads along the edge of the hairpin curves, or it felt that way. Several times the driver stopped the car to show us the scenery. That was even more nerve-racking as the curves were blind and the only way to know if a car was coming was to blast the horn seconds before rounding the curve. We drove into a little town that had a huge painted wooden angel standing beside the door to a building. This was a gallery exhibiting the work of many of the folk artists that we had hoped to meet at the museum. Joyce was thrilled and bought several pieces that we still have in our dining room. Later that evening, we celebrated at a reception in our honour with all the people who were responsible for our visit, and who made it such a rich experience.

In 1989, while I was on sabbatical doing research on pastel drawings and studying paper making, Aboriginal community organizer Daniel Bork approached me with a suggestion to work with inmates on an animation film project about the prevention of drug abuse, at the La Macaza Detention Institute, about 200km north of Montreal. Northern communities were facing an epidemic of residents sniffing toxic substances such as gasoline and glue. In the beginning, Daniel suggested that his prison project should be an animation workshop, but after we talked about it we decided it should be a film project instead. La Macaza is a medium security detention institute located near Mont-Tremblant and houses about 250 inmates, many of whom are Indigenous and Inuit. Not knowing much about substance abuse, I became intrigued and wanted to know more. Over the course of a year, I made many visits to the penitentiary to work with a group of seven Inuit and seven Indigenous men and discuss the effects of sniffing gasoline.

In the beginning, during each visit Daniel and I took notes, and one of the inmates would make drawings that eventually became the storyboard for the film, *The Sniffing Bear/L'ours renifleur* (1992). It was based on a situation that had happened in the North. There was a story coming out of Churchill, Manitoba about polar bears coming to the dump to get food. The local Inuit chased them away, but the persistent bears would always come back. It was because of the gasoline. They would sniff gasoline. They would turn over the skidoos to get at the gas tank and tear apart the jerry cans. They had to shoot some bears, and the others were relocated elsewhere. The story I wanted to tell was of a polar bear becoming addicted to sniffing gasoline. In the end of our film, the bear walks away and we are left with the question of whether he would come back or not.

Instead of making the film with puppets, I made paper cut-outs based on contour drawings and placed them in a 3-D environment. We made the whole film with handmade cotton paper, a craft I had learned in Boston from Elaine Koretsky at Carriage House Paper. I loved making paper and made several large artworks that still grace the walls at home. I also used handmade paper to make trophies for that year's Ottawa International Animation Festival. Two of my other works were also bought by the Cambridge Art Gallery in Ontario.

The Inuit inmates did the preparations for the design and the storyboard for the film at La Macaza, but most of the artwork and all the filming was done in Montreal. First, the pencil drawings were traced onto handmade paper. Then we tore away the contours of the drawings by hand, leaving a silhouette animal with a slightly rough and fluffy edge. The bottom line of the cut-out animals was cut away with a sharp exacto knife, leaving a smooth surface for support and registration. To create a lively texture, the drawings were exchanged every second or third frame. Each drawing was supported in the back by pins and Plexiglas cubes. To see the owl flying, I either used the Plexiglas cubes, or attached very thin wire to the owl to suspend it in the air.

I built a special device to which I attached the wire for winding the owl up or down. I have used this device in all my films. When the animals were supposed to turn around, I took the paper cut-outs out of the set and folded them by hand into a small curve, then placed them back in the set to continue the animation. Every second frame, I folded the animals a little more to make them turn around, creating the effect of a 3-D puppet film. At the outset, we hoped that the inmates would be able to help cut out the drawings and be a part of the filmmaking process, but unfortunately, this did not work out. Some of the inmates had dropped out of the project, so I took the entire artwork home to finish the task myself.

The ice-flows in the background were also made of handmade paper. I would lay full sheets of paper on the surface of a table and then punch a hole in the paper to make a breathing hole for a seal character. The rough edges of the paper created natural shapes that formed the ice flows. Sometimes we had to cut the edges to accentuate the ridges. I loved working with the cotton handmade paper because of its softness and pleasant texture. It was my intention to do the soundtrack with the same inmates from the prison as well, but by the time I was ready to record the music at the prison, the guards were on strike and we couldn't go inside. Instead, I found a terrific composer, Guy Trépanier, in Montreal who composed music for guitar and drum that was very appropriate for the film. There was neither dialogue nor narration, just music and effects.

One morning, I was invited by the local CBC radio station in Montreal to talk about the film. This was at the peak of the toxic gasoline-sniffing crisis in Davis Inlet, Labrador. Phone-in callers expressed their opinion about sniffing glue and gasoline. Some callers were critical of the story, saying that rather than preventing sniffing, the film would encourage people to start. However, the general consensus was that the film could help to make people aware of the perils of sniffing, and it was appreciated everywhere it was shown.

During that time, I developed an interest in the environment, particularly about global warming. This was all over the news, you could not escape it. In the early nineties, there was a growing awareness of global warming and climate change.

Ecosystems were changing and the weather was becoming more and more erratic. I felt I could contribute by making a film about this subject.

The Garden of Ecos/Le jardin d'Écos is a story about an ecosystem that goes out of whack. Again, the sets and characters were made entirely with handmade paper. Denis Rondeau helped with the papermaking and building of the backgrounds. The entire studio floor was covered with elements from the film, and sometimes this made it hard to move around without stepping on the artwork. Some of the scenes in the film required smoke and fumes. This was the first time I used computer generated imaging (CGI) to create these effects. Little insects that drop out of the sky were created by computer and stop-motion animation as well. This was the end of an era. 35mm and 16mm films were slowly fazed out and replaced by video and digital filmmaking. No more heavy equipment to haul around. Everything was lightweight and most visual effects could now be done in-camera. Instead of using optical printers, major special effects could now be done on a laptop computer with instant results.

During my research, I went to the UK and worked with Mark Roberts who specialized in building user-friendly Motion Control units for live-action and animation film productions. I acquired a computerized Motion Control system using a remodelled Panther dolly. With their Flare computer system, I could now use Motion Control for all the camera work in my future films. This saved me a lot of time and energy setting up the camera shots. I could program all the camera movements on the computer. No more need for the labour intensive camera setups and manual planning for each shot. All the movements could be done with the click of a button. With the introduction and rapid development of video,

DVD and digital filmmaking, the demand for film developing services had dwindled to a trickle. Now everything was becoming digital, no more film, except for some animation movies.

In 1999, I was invited to attend the Bibiana Festival in Slovakia. I was to be honoured with a lifetime achievement award, the Prix Klingsor. The legend is that the good magician, Klingsor, on his way to the west, became very tired and needed to rest. When he passed the castle on the mountain near Bratislava, he took the part of the castle with the four towers, turned it upside down and used it as a chair to rest. You can still see the chair on top of the castle. Prix Klingsor is a beautiful sculpture that I proudly keep at home. Receiving this award was very special to me. However, when I came home and showed it to the NFB staff, the reaction was lukewarm. There were no celebrations of any kind.

At this time, the NFB/ONF was faced with severe budget cuts. This led to program restructuring, which greatly affected production output and services. There was no need for laboratory service anymore. The laboratory and all its employees were eliminated. The glorious Golden Years were about to come to a crashing end. In the past, there had been several reports and studies about the ONF/NFB. The biggest one was the Applebaum-Hebert report, which was critical of spending and program management. In the private sector, commercial success rules the market, with the belief being that the more money a film makes the better it is, regardless of content.

Filmmakers were laid off, and it became more difficult to get projects off the ground. The once mighty NFB/ONF with its 1,400 full-time employees was drastically curtailed. Regional and overseas offices closed or could only offer minimal services, and development and research were gone. Now there were no more in-house camera services, and film-makers were taken out of the creative process. Meanwhile, producers became more and more powerful. In the end, there were roughly 450 employees left on staff. Even then, some employees were criticized as being dead wood. Management and producers argued that change was essential for the NFB/ONF to keep up with the times and technological changes.

When I knocked on the door of the NFB in the early sixties, the film industry in Canada was still very small, and film schools were nonexistent. I walked right in and the Film Board welcomed me with open arms. If I had to apply to the NFB/ONF today, I am not sure if they would hire me. The film board is trying to keep up with the changing times. However, because of restructuring, the creative process has suffered dramatically. No more hiring of people on staff. Now animators are hired as freelancers to do a film project and that's it. The private sector works very much this way.

Ludovic the Bear

Most of us had a stuffed animal or doll that was our special friend when we were very young. I remember a well-worn old teddy bear from my childhood. For those of us who somehow lost that special friend along the way, the pang of loss can endure for a lifetime.

One day, a friend's child lost her favourite doll, a teddy bear. She was inconsolable. It gave me the idea of making a story about a teddy bear who finds and saves a small doll who is lost in a snowbank. The lost doll is cold and damaged. "I'll take care of you," the teddy bear promises. This idea first grew into the film *Ludovic, The Snow Gift/Ludovic, Une poupée dans la neige* (1998), which was followed by three more seasonal Ludovic stories; and later an international TV series with the same main character Ludovic, produced in the private sector.

In the beginning, I had no name for the teddy bear. Then Marie-Francine Hébert, who was the scriptwriter for the film, remembered that her grandfather was called Ludovic. I liked it, and that is how the bear got his name. My grandchildren,

Aaron and Ariel, were still very young at this time and seeing them at play inspired me a lot for the Ludovic characters. They were very close and always kind to each other.

For the design of Ludovic, I made some rough sketches based on my childhood teddy bear and gave them to Lilian Kruip who made the puppets. I also provided her with the armatures that she would insert inside them.

For close to two years, I worked with three different producers to make the Ludovic film. Thérèse Descary worked on the film until she retired, then Jean-Jacques Leduc took over her job, and finally Michèle Bélanger was in charge. After seeing the first screening of Ludovic, The Snow Gift/ Ludovic, Une poupée dans la neige, Michèle mentioned in the corridor that she already wanted to see more Ludovic films. This was not my intention, because I had other creative ideas I was planning to pursue next. "What about covering the four seasons, each with its own Ludovic adventure?" Michèle insisted. Reluctantly, I accepted the idea as long as we could speed up the production process. We agreed that each of the next three films should take less than a year to make.

For each successive film, I worked with small teams of two or three people at a time. Among them were: Lilian Kruip for the making of the Ludovic dolls and the design of all the other puppets; Joyce Ryckman for her artistic advice and continuity; Denis Rondeau designed and built the sets; and Chantal Masson, Sylvie Chartrand and Éric Bolté helped with the animation in the studio. Marie-Francine Hébert became the scriptwriter for the mini series. Sometimes Marie-Francine and I would get stuck on the actions we were writing. We would take a break and then continue writing again, which seemed to always solve the problem. We would then happily finish writing the scene for the day, and then move on the next morning.

Daniel Lavoie composed the music for the Ludovic films. On several occasions, I went to visit him in his studio and listened to the compositions in progress. I liked his approach to the film and the sensitivities he underlined in the visuals with his compositions. His music worked well with the films. The result was outstanding, and added to the quality of the four films.

The other films in the mini series were called: *Ludovic, A Crocodile in my Garden/Ludovic, Un crocodile dans mon jardin* (2000); *Ludovic, Visiting Grandpa/Des vacance chez grand-papa* (2001); and *Ludovic, Magic in the Air/Un vent de magie* (2002). The four films became very popular, winning more than 22 awards, including the Radio-Canada Le Prix d'excellence for *Ludovic, The Snow Gift/Ludovic, une poupée dans la neige*. The four films could be watched on their own, or as a group, which was collectively released as *Four Seasons in the Life of Ludovic/Quatre saisons dans la vie de Ludovic* (2002). The 46-minute compilation made it into many major children's film festivals, and also enjoyed a theatrical release.

In France, the film became very popular and was shown widely in theatres. Many times, I was invited to accompany the film to festivals. The children in Norway brought their own teddy bears to the theatre to greet me. I got the same teddy bear reception at the public library in Chicago. Children and their parents stood in line outside the theatre waiting to greet me and Ludovic, and to sign autographs. It was heart-warming to see children in the theatre holding up their little bears. After the screenings, the kids made drawings of Ludovic.

After the *Ludovic* films were completed, Roger Rotis in the Distribution Department suggested that the NFB have a float for the Santa Clause Parade featuring Ludovic. I thought this was a super idea and that my grandchildren should participate. André Vien of Théâtre Sans Fil designed the mascot and was also the puppeteer. The parade took place in Montreal and started at the bottom of Dorchester street. I had invited my children and their kids to take part in the parade. Unfortunately, it was very cold and they took turns warming up inside the little hut on the float.

A few years later, I was working on a project called *Marianne's Theatre/Le théâtre de Marianne* with Sylvie Chartrand when the NFB/ONF's head of studio Marcel Jean and lead administrator came into the animation studio to make a big announcement. Cité Amérique had bought the rights from the ONF to produce *Ludovic, the Television Series/Ludovic, La série télévision* (2008 - 2011), consisting of 26 episodes for television. I had no idea that this was happening, and I was quite upset to hear that the ONF/NFB had sold the rights to the private sector without telling me first. They made it sound as if I had just won the lottery, but I was not impressed. For them, it was a big deal that would eventually bring in some hard needed cash. They went ahead anyway.

Even though I thought it was a stupid idea, I conceded that it could work if the producers accepted certain conditions. Ludovic should keep his original shape and character; there must be respect for the sensitivities in the original stories; and there should be no lip-sync dialogue with the other puppets, because that would change the dynamics too much. None of what I suggested was accepted. The series became a big co-production between Canada, Germany, The Netherlands and

Bulgaria. There was a large team of scriptwriters, storyboard artists and consultants involved. Each had their own say in the project. There were often disagreements among the producers from Canada and Germany about the structure and content of the series. Everything was scrutinized and taken apart.

The main investor was from Germany. He had his own priorities that did not always please me. One big stumbling block was lip-syncing the dialogue. We had many other disagreements, and the producers would argue about it at great length. It was all done through correspondence between Canada and Germany.

To make the series suitable for TV, they felt that the story lines had to be drastically modified with more dramatic development, dynamic action, dialogue, lip-sync and movable mouths. Even the film sets were completely modified to suit the series. All this affected the final outcome considerably. In the process, Ludovic lost a lot of his original charm. I had my conflicts with the Canadian producers as well. I was supposed to be the principal director, but often the work was not to the satisfaction of my producers. In the end, I had to resign as director, but stayed on as script consultant for the 26 episodes.

Ludovic the series did not get the worldwide distribution for television the producers had hoped for. However, the episodes were very much appreciated wherever they were shown. Children in Holland enjoyed the TV series, and were always looking forward to the next episode, even if it was a repeat. The series was also shown on CBC and Radio-Canada, in Germany, and other European countries.

I still prefer the four original *Ludovic* films I made at the Film Board. I don't believe that making the films more dramatic and dynamic for television audiences made them better. If I had to do it all over again, I would fight a lot harder to preserve the original quality and character of my kind old bear: Ludovic.

The Puppet Master

Perhaps you have read *Pinocchio*, the story of the mischievous puppet that eventually became a boy? Pinocchio is a marionette, but there are many types of puppets: finger puppets, glove puppets, shadow puppets, marionettes, and even objects such as blocks can be used as puppets. I find puppets magical. They trigger my imagination. There are so many things you can do in puppetry that you cannot do in real life, but the manipulation requires skill.

Marianne's Theatre/Le théâtre de Marianne came about when I was invited to attend a Children's Festival in Mexico to give talks to a number of theatre groups on the differences between theatrical puppetry and stop-motion puppetry. Puppet theatre performers work directly in view of the public, while for puppet films all the action is planned beforehand and recorded on film. While there, I saw many puppet theatre performances and that inspired me a lot. Not all shows were smooth sailing. I recall one time the string puppets became all tangled up. On stage, the puppeteer unraveled the strings and the show went on as before. This I found fascinating, and it inspired me to make a film about it.

The inspiration for the film was already clear in my mind when I was in Mexico. Back in Montreal, I discussed the idea of making a film about acrobats doing all kinds of performances until something goes wrong, and who is in charge—the puppet master or the puppets—with my producer Thérèse Descary, and that is how we started.

We hired Marie-Pierre Simard from a puppet theatre group to design Marianne. After that, Sylvie Chartrand came on board to help me with the animation. She did a terrific job. However, she had other work as well, and was not always available. During these times, I continued on my own. I also worked with Éric Bolté, but that did not work out. We had no other people, except for Olivier Calvert the sound designer, and Robert M. Lepage who composed the original music. All the other puppets (the acrobats), I made myself. The theatre was designed by Denis Rondeau.

The actual stop motion animation was done by Sylvie and myself. The most challenging part was the trapeze with the acrobats flying in the air. To do it well, I looked at films with real circus acrobats to work out the timing of the action. The actual animation of the acrobats was done with strings attached to the puppets and pulled by pulleys away from the camera to make it all invisible.

Marianne's Theatre/Le théâtre de Marianne was my last film before retiring from the Film Board. The reason to retire was purely an administrative decision; I had no choice. The NFB only wanted to continue with freelancers, and all permanent staff were laid off. When the film was finished, it was very well received. After this experience, I was ready to carry on with my next project, which would bring me into uncharted waters.

Near the end of 1999, Japanese animator and puppet master, Kihachirō Kawamoto, arranged an invitation by the Japan Foundation for me to come to Japan as a visiting artist. It was an offer I could not refuse. I was in the middle of working on the film *Ludovic, Visiting Grandpa/Ludovic, Des vacance chez grandpapa.* I put it on the shelf for two months and hopped a plane to Japan.

While there, 'Chiro' and I were invited to the Hiroshima International Animation Festival. We took the Shinkansen bullet train from Tokyo to Hiroshima at 250 mph. It was a pleasant ride and one did not feel the train accelerating. The only regret I had was that we would not see Mount Fuji because it was overcast. The couple of hours travelling passed by like a blur. The ride was smooth and it was not too crowded. It felt very comfortable. There were other animators travelling with us that made it even more pleasant.

When I was in Japan, I visited the Hiroshima Peace Memorial Museum with Suzanne Gervais, whose film was being shown in the festival. We saw terrible artefacts from the bombing of Hiroshima. Pictures of burning skin, shadows of victims on walls, clocks, lunch boxes, clothing, and hair. One display held the remains of a red tricycle that once belonged to a three-year-old boy named Shinichi. He and a little girl were playing with his tricycle at 8:16 a.m. on August 6, 1945, when the bomb exploded. In an instant, 80,000 people died, including the boy and the little girl. Years later, workers found and returned the wrecked tricycle to Shinichi's father. He brought it to the museum where it has been on display ever since. A book and film were made about the boy and his tricycle, and I thought the story could also make a terrific animated film. The horrific damage that war does to children has formed an essential part of my life from my earliest days during the Nazi occupation of Holland.

For a long time I wanted to make a film about children and war. Only after I left the NFB did I find time to focus on *55 Socks* again. My idea was submitted to Michèle Bélanger, and she allowed me to prepare a storyboard. Many years before, I had already worked out ideas about making this film in silhouettes, but I revised my plans and made a new storyboard. Joyce suggested that the poem be set between two newscasts, one a war report and the other near the end of the war, which would clearly set the time period.

While I was working on the storyboard for *55 Socks*, Laurie Gordon was working on a documentary about the animator Ryan Larkin, my old co-worker on *Running Time*. She asked if she could interview me for the film. At the end of my interview for Laurie's film, I told her that I was looking for a producer to help me with *55 Socks*, and she gladly took on the job.

Laurie was taking care of Ryan in her home while he worked on a new film called Spare Change about his panhandling days on the streets of Montreal. He had an addictive personality, and his drug and alcohol use was a problem for him, even back in the seventies. Ryan never finished his film. Other animators finished the project. At the time when Ryan worked at the NFB, he made some brilliant films such as *Walking/En marchant* (1968) and *Street Musique* (1972). He had followed therapy in the past to overcome his problems, but it did not work out. He was already in trouble and had to leave the Film Board. Sometimes he sent for a taxi to pick up his pay cheque. That did not go over very well. His addiction got out of hand, and in the end he lived as a homeless person on the streets of Montreal, panhandling. At the same time, Ryan had a very pleasant personality. People liked being around him, but were not able to help him. Eventually, he developed cancer, and passed away a few years later.

As *55 Socks* progressed, we met many times at Laurie's home in St. Hyacinth to work out the ideas for the visuals as well as the soundtrack. Since *55 Socks* was a co-production, some of the work was to be done in The Netherlands. The Dutch producer, Peter Lindhout, was in charge of preparing the soundtrack in Amsterdam. Laurie composed the music in Montreal, then joined us in Holland while we prepared the final mix.

I stayed with my nephew Joost in Amsterdam. I borrowed one of his bikes and I felt right at home cycling in Amsterdam. On a windy day on my way to the recording studio, I cycled up the ramp of a bridge when suddenly the wind turned and I rode straight into another cyclist who was carrying a large load of wood. Everything went flying, including my computer. Luckily, there was no damage and nobody was injured, but there was wood all over the bridge. Bystanders helped us get up on our feet and cleaned up the mess. Of course I blamed it on the wind.

During her stay in The Netherlands, Laurie discovered that herring is a real Dutch treat and she fell in love with it. To please her appetite, one morning I offered to buy some herring for a snack. She didn't want just one or two fish, she wanted a whole dozen. Laurie protested my argument that twelve herring was too many, and that it would make her sick: "Oh yes, I will eat them all," she promised. If not, she would finish them the following day on the train going to Germany. In the end she managed to eat two and shared one more with a friend. I believe the leftover herring landed on the railroad tracks somewhere between Holland and Germany.

Two more silhouette animation films completed my trilogy on children and war: *The Blue Marble/La bille bleue* (2014), and *The Cardinal/Le cardinal* (2016). The many stories about child soldiers I had heard and read about gave me the idea to make a film about children trained as child soldiers. In *The Blue Marble/La bille bleue*, village children are kidnapped from their school by plundering insurgents and are driven to training camps in the jungle to be trained as child soldiers. The girl in the story has a blue marble. It acts as a charm to protect her and the other children when danger arrives. One night when the intoxicated child soldiers are searching the bushes ready to attack, a bullet destroys the blue marble and the spell is broken.

Marie-Josée Saint-Pierre was my producer. In the beginning, it all went very smoothly. However, she was also very much involved in making her own film about Claude Jutra. Near the end of finishing *The Blue Marble/La bille bleue*, she had very little time to help me out with my production. That left me completely on my own. In order to speak to her, I had to make an appointment. I considered this to be disrespectful, insulting, and contrary to our work agreement. I refused. Being left on my own I felt abandoned, but I continued as best as I could, and it did not make a difference to the final outcome of the film.

Roméo Dallaire, the Canadian general and senator, inspired me a lot with his experience peacekeeping in Rwanda.

He had written several books on the subject of child soldiers, and he kindly wrote a letter of support for my film. When we applied for funding, I asked Joyce to write a poem for the storyboard. Joyce had a big influence in the making of the film, she believed very strongly in what I was doing. She encouraged me to carry on with the project about children and war.

Bird-watching with my daughter Anouk inspired me to make *The Cardinal/Le cardinal.* Anouk had developed an interest in bird watching that led to collecting and caring for birds that had flown into windows. Almost every day she would get calls about injured birds. Eventually she started a group called Safe Wings and became an official bird resuscitator. The top floor of her house turned into a bird hospital. Now if I want to visit her, it feels like I have to be a bird to get in the door. Sometimes Anouk and I would go bird watching together. One time a cardinal flew around us, and that gave me the idea to make a film with a cardinal.

Instead of placing this film in a war zone, T*he Cardinal/Le cardinal* was mainly about the friendship between a red bird and a little girl. The girl's father was a soldier and served in Afghanistan. One day, the father gave a chocolate bar to an Afghan girl. Moments later, she was killed by a car bomb, and died in his arms. Another time, the father witnessed a soldier friend being struck and killed by an exploding bomb. When the father returns home, he is easily irritated, loses his pre-war interest in bird-watching, becomes aggressive, starts drinking, and ends up homeless. The story ends with the cardinal helping the girl find her dad, and she helps him seek help for PTSD.

For the first time in my career, I realized I was going to have to produce a film as well as direct it. All expenses for the film were paid out of my pocket, so working at home with no overhead saved me a lot of money. The film became a family affair: Joyce wrote the narrative, Jessica did the English voice of the young girl, and I did the animation, directing and producing. I couldn't use high-standing tripods or animation stands because my basement clearance was too low, so I built a complete camera unit that I attached upside down to the ceiling. The north-south, east-west movements of the camera were done manually, turning tiny wheels that moved the camera. The zooms were done with a zoom lens by simply winding up or down a waxed string that was attached to it. All the digital recordings and visual effects were done on the computer.

I enjoyed working at home with my camera contraption and the digital camera; it was simple and pretty efficient. This way of working was impossible in the past with the old heavy 35mm film cameras. At one point we had a basement flood, and I was able to move all my home equipment to the NFB/ONF and continue the animation there. I constructed a frame on the wall of the studio to which I attached my upside down camera contraption. After years of absence, I once again found myself in familiar surroundings at the NFB. Every day, people dropped by to say hello and were curious to know what I was up to. Four months later, I returned home to the pleasant tranquility of my renovated basement studio. I must admit that sometimes I got a little lonely down there on my own.

During post-production, I was invited back to Japan for a work-visit with students, and I decided to take the unfinished film with me. When I showed *The Cardinal/Le cardinal* rough cut to the students at the University of the Arts in Yokohama, animator Koji Yamamura and his co-coordinator Ilan Nguyen offered to do the music and sound effects with the help of the music department at Tokyo University for the Arts, free of charge.

In 2016, I returned to Japan to work on the sound for the film. They did a terrific job doing the sound effects and the music for the film, and I happily went home with the final mix. In the end, Le conseil des Arts et des lettres du Québec gave me a grant of $10,000 for post-production, and the NFB/ONF helped with the finishing of the film at a minimal cost. The two films, T*he Blue Marble/La bille bleue* and *The Cardinal/Le cardinal*, are distributed by Vidéographe, Montreal, with Denis Vaillancourt in charge of distribution.

When I returned from Japan after the film's final mix, I had a lot of pain in my back. I was diagnosed with crushed vertebrae as well as Multiple Myeloma. It was then that I retired from filmmaking to focus on my health. I was not sure if this would be my last film. My health was my priority. Being at home there was no more influence from the outside world. To be creative again took a lot of energy. That kind of energy I just did not have anymore. I did not get any more opportunities to teach or do workshops; it all disappeared, and I lost contact with the animation world. *The Cardinal/Le cardinal* was my final film. Joyce supported me all the way, and as I was either sleeping or sitting around passing time, she encouraged me to write this memoirs.

At that time, I was not ready to retire and wanted to continue making films. But then I started to get back pains that interfered with thinking clearly, so I had to stop. This worried me quite a bit. When my twin brother, Ferry, visited us in Montreal in 2008, he struggled a lot with his memory.

For instance, he would forever look for his wallet and his cellphone. My sister, Ans, came along on that visit to keep him company and to keep an eye on him because she was quite concerned about his memory loss. At one point Ans thought he was suffering from Alzheimer's and notified everyone in the family. This did not go over well, and everybody was upset because it was still a rumour. After his visit with us, Ferry went to see a specialist in Holland who confirmed that indeed he was already in the advanced stages of Alzheimer's. Soon after, he could no longer stay at home and was admitted to the Lisiduna hof in Leusden. He stayed there for about two years until he died in 2014. I went to his funeral and paid tribute to his rich life as a sculptor. One of his works still graces the hall of the Piet Mondriaan museum in Amersfoort.

When I started in filmmaking, everything we did was done in black and white. Only in the early sixties when colour film was introduced did we change to use colour. Often, I preferred black and white films. At that time, we could easily manipulate the images, change the grey scale and increase the contrast, to be more in tune with the film. This was always done on the original negative. It was always a team effort. At that time, we did not have optical printers. Film studios in Holland are not very numerous, and most of them concentrate on advertisement and television productions. For the production of feature films, it is a different story.

In Canada, the private sector has taken over for the NFB. It is a thriving industry that has many outlets. We can see everything on our computers, iPads, and smartphones. The opportunities to work in this media are big. Many times, the animator plays a small part in the production. The producers are more involved with the whole process. After my retirement from the

NFB, when I started to make independent films, the first thing I had to produce was a storyboard, then to find a producer and the money to make the film. This is no easy task. After this, I needed a production studio in which to film. The filming can be done alone by the animator, but collaboration is definitely needed for post production.

Digital filmmaking is the way of the future, but that may change again over time. Studios rely a lot on collaboration, from script writers to set designers, background artists, animators, camera crews, and editors. Often the work is farmed out to other countries where it is less expensive to produce. With the exception of some traditional animation, everything now is digital and computer generated.

I am grateful for the opportunities that I found in Canada. For the most part, I was able to make films with financial security and little creative interference at the ONF/NFB. The French Animation department at the ONF has been most supportive of me, particularly under the guidance of René Jodoin, the founder of the studio.

In 2003, the Cinémathèque Québeçoise organized a retrospective exhibition of my films and film sets, titled *The Garden of Childhood,* to commemorate their 40th anniversary. Following its six-month stay in Montreal, the exhibition travelled to Le château d'Annecy in France for another six months. Over the years, my films and film sets have been shown in exhibitions at the Montreal Museum of Fine Arts, Le Musée d'art de Joliette, The Musée de la civilisation in Quebec City, various cultural centres in Quebec and Ontario, and the MOMA in New York City, as well as the Canadian Cultural Centre in Paris, France.

I loved my career as an animation filmmaker that started in Holland when I replied to a simple ad in the paper. Little did I know that it would bring me so much acclaim and success. I have followed my dreams and persisted in my vision of what I wanted to accomplish in film. Although I have adjusted to the digital format of filmmaking, I am still nostalgic for manual 35mm film cameras, editing machines, and setting up each shot frame by frame. Who knows what the future will bring, but I still find charm in the old ways of stop-motion filmmaking.

Acknowledgements

Writing this book came about soon after I retired from filmmaking in 2017. I was recovering from Multiple Myeloma and was not strong enough to concentrate on making films. It was my wife, Joyce Ryckman, who encouraged me to look at my notes and writings of the many anecdotes I had collected about my life, films, and travels. She became my mentor, and her input made the book what it is today. Thank you, Joyce!

A number of people have helped along the way. Thanks to Dorota Kosinska who read the first draft and added suggestions, Peter Hays who read the second draft, and deftly pulled it apart and put it back together. Thanks, too, to Matt Hays for suggesting his brother Peter. Also invaluable were Anthony and Anne Kent, my daughter Anouk Hoedeman, and my sister Hetty Kroese for reading the manuscript, or parts thereof, and making suggestions. My thanks also goes to my step daughter, Jessica Blair, who solidly supported the book from the beginning and enriched it with her photographs. Also thanks to Janice Johnson for the terrific photo of Joyce and me at the

Fête Nationale. Gratitude to Michael Blair and Pamela Hilliard for their support, encouragement and professional advice (Michael is a writer) and, of course, to my family in Canada and The Netherlands, who have stood by me throughout this project and my career.

I also want to acknowledge the National Film Board of Canada without whose support of my career this book could not have been written.

I am indebted to Nina Lee McIntyre for leading me through the stages of the final book, and to Matt Joudrey for taking a chance on me and publishing *Frame by Frame, An Animator's Journey.* Dank U! Thank you!

Filmography

2016 The Cardinal/Le cardinal
(Writer, Director, Producer, Animator)
Silhouette animation

2014 The Blue Marble/La bille bleue
(Writer, Director, Producer, Animator)
Silhouette animation

2011 55 Socks/55 Chaussettes/55 Sokken
(Writer, Director, Animator)
Silhouette animation

2008 - 2011
Ludovic, the Television Series/Ludovic, La série télévision (Creator, Director, Consultant)
Digital animation

2004 Marianne's Theatre/Le théâtre de Marianne
(Writer, Director, Animator)
Glove puppet, 3D cut-outs, and live-action

2003 Winter Days/Jours d'hiver
(Animator, Director)
3D cut-outs

2002 Four Seasons in the Life of Ludovic/Quatre saisons dans la vie de Ludovic, (Writer, Director, Animator)
3D puppets

2002 Ludovic, Magic in the Air/Ludovic, Un vent de magie, (Writer, Director, Animator)
3D puppets

2001 Ludovic, Visiting Grandpa/Des vacances chez grand-papa (Writer, Director, Animator)
3D puppets

2000 Ludovic, A Crocodile in my Garden/Ludovic, Un crocodile dans mon jardin
(Writer, Director, Animator)
3D puppets

1998 Ludovic, the Snow Gift/Ludovic, Une poupée dans la neige (Writer, Director, Animator)
3D puppets

1997 The Garden of Ecos/Le jardin d'Écos
(Writer, Director, Animator)
Handmade paper cut-outs

1992 The Sniffing Bear/L'ours renifleur
(Writer, Director, Animator)
Handmade paper cut-outs

1989 The Box/La boîte
(Writer, Director, Animator)
Illustrated 3D cut-outs, live-action

1987 Charles and François/Charles et François
(Writer, Director, Animator)
Illustrated 3D cut-outs

1984 Mascarade/Mascarade
(Writer, Director, Animator)
Papier maché 3D puppets

1980 Treasure of the Grotoceans/ Le Trésor des Grotocéans
(Writer, Director, Animator)
Papier maché 3D puppets

1980 Co Hoedeman, Animator
(Actor, Animator)
Foam puppet, mixed-media, live-action

1977 The Sand Castle/Le château de sable
(Writer, Director, Animator)
Sand, foam puppets coated with sand

1975 Monsieur Pointu
(Cameraman)
Pixelation

1975 The Man and the Giant, an Eskimo Legend/L'homme et le géant, une légende Eskimo
(Writer, Director, Animator)
Soapstone carvings, live-action

1975 Lumaaq, an Eskimo Legend/Lumaaq, une légende Eskimo (Writer, Director, Animator)
Cut out shapes of ink drawings

1974 Running Time
(Animator)
Mixed-media

1973 The Owl and the Raven, an Eskimo Legend/Le hibou et le corbeau, une légende Eskimo
(Writer, Director, Animator)
3D puppets made from traditional Inuit materials

1972 Tchou-tchou/Tchou-tchou
(Writer, Director, Animator)
Illustrated wooden blocks

1971 The Owl and the Lemming, an Eskimo Legend/Le hibou et le lemming, une légende Eskimo
(Writer, Director, Animator)
3D puppets made from traditional Inuit materials

1970 Matrioska/Matrioska
(Writer, Director, Animator)
Russian nesting dolls

1969 Oddball/Maboule
(Writer, Director, Animator)
Pipe cleaner puppet, styrofoam and cork balls

1968 Continental Drift/La dérive des continents
(Director, Animator)
Mixed-media

1967 The Skeleton/Le skelet
(Animator)
Mixed-media

Documentary Films About Co Hoedeman

2013 Making Movie History: Co Hoedeman/Une histoire du cinéma: Co Hoedeman
Directed by Denys Desjardins

1996 In the Animator's Eye: A Conjurer's Tale – Co Hoedeman
Directed by Isabelle-Monique Turcotte

1980 Co Hoedeman, Animator/Co Hoedeman, Animateur
Directed by Nico Crama